Annuals for
EveryGarden

Scott D. Appell

EDITOR

Janet Marinelli
SERIES EDITOR

Sigrun Wolff Saphire
SENIOR EDITOR

Mark C. Tebbitt
SCIENCE EDITOR

Leah Kalotay
ART DIRECTOR

Steven Clemants
VICE-PRESIDENT,
SCIENCE & PUBLICATIONS

Judith D. Zuk
PRESIDENT

Elizabeth Scholtz
DIRECTOR EMERITUS

Handbook #174

Copyright © 2003 by Brooklyn Botanic Garden, Inc.

All-Region Guides, formerly *21st-Century Gardening Series,* are
published three times a year at 1000 Washington Ave.,
Brooklyn, NY 11225.

Subscription included in Brooklyn Botanic Garden subscriber
membership dues ($35 per year; $45 outside the United States).

ISBN # 1-889538-57-4

Printed by Science Press, a division of the Mack Printing Group.
Printed on recycled paper.

Cover: *Consolida ajacis,* larkspur.
Above: An annual planting features zinnias and larkspurs.

Annuals for Every Garden
Table of Contents

Mad About Annuals 4

Encyclopedia of Annuals 9

    Delightful Daisies 10

    Long-Lasting Flowers 17

    Edible Annuals 23

    Annuals With Fabulous Foliage 31

    Evening Bloomers 36

    Morning Glories and Their Relatives 42

    Annuals for Picking 49

    Annuals for Shade 61

    Tender Tropicals 68

    Drought-Tolerant Bloomers 76

    Sensational Salvias 83

    More Recommendations 89

Growing Basics 91

A Step-by-Step Guide to Propagation 96

For More Information 103

Mail-Order Sources 104

Contributors 105

Index 107

Mad About Annuals

Scott D. Appell

Light-years ago, when I was renting a small house in Columbus, Ohio, while continuing my graduate studies in horticulture, I made a momentous discovery. I fell madly in love with annuals. I realized that by using these plants I could perennially (no pun intended) transform the plantings on my quarter-acre property. I could modify the color combinations willy-nilly, create ever-changing garden designs, devote entire beds, borders, or containers to annuals with specific purposes: blooms destined for fresh-cut flower arrangements, for example, or candidates for dried floral designs intended as holiday gifts. When I was forced to work a third-shift job to augment my meager student budget, I created an evening garden and delighted in its nocturnal beauty and fragrance. And when I had major travel plans, no problem— I'd devise a planting of drought-resistant annual beauties. Ever since, I have experimented with newly introduced annuals at my caprice, every single year. Annuals have long been called "the gardener's palette" by virtue of not only their versatility but also their infinite variety of colors and forms. Annuals make it possible for any gardener to become a horticultural Vincent van Gogh.

During the decades since my grad school days, there have been enormous changes in the world of annuals. Intensive breeding programs, extensive cultural trials, and the advent of tissue culture have brought us innumerable exciting new varieties. At the same time, the term "annual" is being used much more liberally, increasing choices even more. A number of confusing variations on the word "annual" have become popular in nursery catalogs and gardening literature. Most are references to plants

Opposite: The flower spikes of pink and purple larkspur, *Consolida ajacis,* frame the showy bright pink blooms of lavatera and clarkia.

used as annuals in the garden, at least in cool climates, but that are not true annuals in the botanical sense of the word.

In order to demystify what qualifies as an "annual plant" these days, let's take a look at the container planting on the facing page, a terra-cotta pot brimming with sensational, cutting-edge annuals. The planting is indeed a magnificent sight to behold, but the botany behind it is as interesting as the plants themselves. They include both true annuals and plants that, technically speaking, are not true annuals but are used as annuals nowadays, especially in cool climates.

True Annuals

The chartreuse-flowered *Zinnia elegans* 'Envy' in our planting is the only example of a true annual. Botanically speaking, annuals are plants that complete their life cycle—growing from seed, flowering, setting seed, and dying—within one growing year.

Hardy Annuals

The snapdragon, *Antirrhinum majus* 'Black Prince', in actuality a short-lived perennial, is known in horticultural circles as a hardy annual because it can tolerate light frost and even a little snow. In fact, when cultivated in warm regions or in a protected site in cooler areas, it can even overwinter and bloom the following year. Dusty miller (*Senecio cineraria*) is often listed in this category as well because it can overwinter quite happily in cool regions.

Half-Hardy Annuals

Plectranthus argentatus, an evergreen shrub native to Australia, is often termed a half-hardy annual by horticulturists; this implies that it can be set back, damaged, or killed by continued exposure to frost, but a few light frosts will not harm it.

Tender Annuals

The coleus, *Solenostemon* 'Palisandra', and the licorice plant, *Helichrysum petiolare*, are all considered tender annuals. Native to warmer parts of the globe, they are killed by the first frost. Of course, in their countries of origin, and in the warmest parts of North America, they are perennial and live more than one year. The taro, dahlia, and ornamental sweet potato are tender annuals too; they are also tuberous plants, which means that in cool climates, after frost has killed their tops, the tubers can be dug up, stored over winter, and replanted when the soil warms up the following spring.

Different Types of Plants Commonly Used in Annual Displays

1. *Solenostemon* 'Palisandra', coleus, tender annual

2. *Plectranthus argentatus*, half-hardy annual

3. *Senecio cineraria*, dusty miller, hardy annual

4. *Colocasia* 'Black Magic', taro, tender annual

5. *Dahlia* 'Bishop of Llandaff', dahlia, tender annual

6. *Zinnia elegans* 'Envy', zinnia, true annual

7. *Antirrhinum majus* 'Black Prince', snapdragon, hardy annual

8. *Furcraea foetida* 'Mediopicta', Mauritius hemp, tender perennial

9. *Ipomoea batatas* 'Pink Frost', sweet potato, tender annual

10. *Helichrysum petiolare*, licorice plant, tender annual

A fabulous combination of colorful annuals enlivens any garden. From left to right, this planting includes *Plectranthus,* zinnias, chard, marigolds, Mexican sunflowers, salvias, dahlias, and petunias.

Tender Perennials

The variegated Mauritius hemp, *Furcraea foetida* 'Mediopicta', is one of another group of plants used as annuals in cool climates, called tender perennials. This horticulturally vague term implies that these plants will flourish happily outdoors during the growing season but need to be overwintered indoors in temperate regions. Like the plants known as tender annuals, they are perennial in their native habitats, where they may grow into huge specimens.

No matter how these plants are categorized, they are all used as annuals in all but the warmest North American climates. They are also some of the most spectacular plants to be cultivated in any situation. So read on and discover how you can use annuals in your garden to become a horticultural Monet or Matisse.

Encyclopedia of Annuals

On the following pages you will find portraits of close to a hundred plants perfect for an annual garden. For easy reference, symbols indicating light requirements, soil moisture, plant height and spread, as well as flower color or other ornamental features appear in a box at the top of each encyclopedia entry. Please check the chart below to find out what the symbols mean. Then read on to find more detailed plant descriptions and growing tips as well as fabulous cultivars and noteworthy relatives of the featured species.

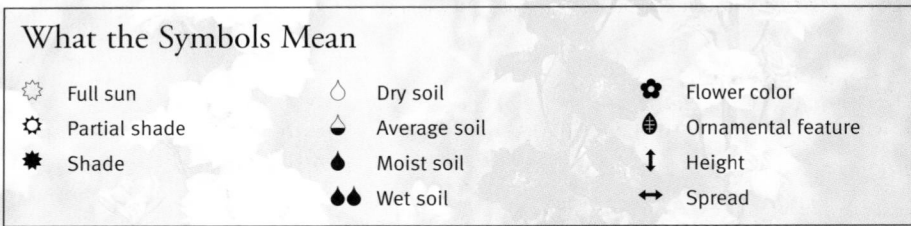

What the Symbols Mean

☼ Full sun	◊ Dry soil	✿ Flower color	
✿ Partial shade	◖ Average soil	◉ Ornamental feature	
✳ Shade	◆ Moist soil	↕ Height	
	◆◆ Wet soil	↔ Spread	

Delightful Daisies

Ask a child to draw a flower and chances are you'll be presented with a daisy lookalike, a central disk surrounded by ray flowers. That's the hallmark of the aster family, Asteraceae, also known as the composite family, Compositae. There's enormous variation of flower color and size in this family—certainly something for everyone.

Bracteantha bracteata (*Helichrysum bracteatum*) • Strawflower

❀ Gold, copper, silver

↕ 24" ↔ 12"; plant 12" apart.

Strawflowers look as if they were spun from precious metals, covering the top of the plant with buttons of color and creating a multihued effect of different-size flower heads. Blossoms are 2 inches wide when fully opened and are excellent for drying, keeping their color for years.

Growing Tips Strawflowers will bloom all summer long, thriving in the heat and self-seeding in sandy soil. Start seeds indoors six to eight weeks before the last frost in your area. If your growing season is at least 16 weeks, you may sow seeds directly in the garden after the danger of frost has passed.

Companion Plants The soft gray foliage of lavender cotton (*Santolina chamaecyparissus*)

Opposite: *Bracteantha bracteata*, strawflower.

offers a muted contrast to the vivid strawflower. For a hot, tropical look, combine it with an equally bright colored *Canna*, such as *C.* 'Pretoria', or one of the brighter shrub verbenas (*Lantana*).

Cultivars and Related Species *Bracteantha bracteata* 'Bronze Gold' and 'Pink' are two metallic beauties. 'Golden Beauty' has bronze flowers with yellow tips.

Calendula officinalis • Pot Marigold

❀ Bright orange, yellow; quieter shades of apricot, yellow, cream

↕ 12"–30" ↔ 12"–18"; plant 8" apart.

Called pot marigold because it was once used in cooking, *Calendula* is not only a good container plant but also makes an easy, colorful groundcover or mass planting. The 2½- to 4½-inch blooms are good for cutting, and the petals can be tossed in salads or sprinkled on rice dishes for a touch of color. The bright green leaves are lance- to spoon-shaped.

Growing Tips This hardy annual prefers cool weather, adapts to most well-drained soils, and will happily self-seed. For spring bloom, start seeds very early indoors and set out as soon as the soil can be worked. For fall or winter bloom in warm regions, sow seeds in place outdoors and thin to 12 inches apart. The cut flowers are long lasting. Pot marigold is very susceptible to powdery mildew.

Companion Plants Purple-flowered sweet alyssum (*Lobularia maritima* 'Oriental Nights') adds a nice contrast to orange pot marigold. The hot colors of *Nemesia strumosa* 'Carnival' Series make pot marigold pop. Good foliage plants to combine with pot marigold include ornamental kale (*Brassica oleracea*) with creamy highlights and parsley (*Petroselinum crispum*).

Cultivars and Related Species Cultivars of *Calendula officinalis* 'Pacific Beauty' Series produce double flower heads in shades of apricot and cream as well as yellow and orange.

Coreopsis tinctoria • Golden Coreopsis

☼ ◑

❀ Mahogany, yellow; yellow tips and mahogany bases

↕ 24"–36" ↔ 12"; plant 12" apart.

The single or double flowers of this annual coreopsis are slightly more than an inch in diameter and work beautifully in cut-flower arrangements. The foliage is feathery and light.

Growing Tips Golden coreopsis is easy to grow and frequently self-sows. Plant seeds outdoors in early spring in well-drained soil; cold weather won't hamper germination. Coreopsis blooms best when crowded, so don't thin seedlings as they grow.

Cosmos bipinnatus 'Sonata', cosmos.

Companion Plants Try *Coreopsis tinctoria* with *Geranium himalayense*. The deep purple-blue flowers of the geranium provide striking contrast to those of this coreopsis. The upright flowers of speedwell (*Veronica virginica* and *V. spicata*) also mix well with the daisy-shaped bloom of *Coreopsis*.

Cultivars and Related Species *Coreopsis tinctoria* 'Mahogany Midget' is a dwarf cultivar with deep red blooms that grows 10 inches tall and wide. Other dwarf cultivars, excellent for containers, include 'Golden Sovereign' and 'Tiger Star'.

Cosmos bipinnatus • Cosmos

☼ ◑

❀ White, pink, magenta, striped

↕ 5'–6' ↔ 18"–24"; plant 18" apart.

Cosmos is an old-fashioned flower but by no means passé. The profuse feathery foliage adds wonderful texture to any garden. Blooms are about 2 inches in diameter. Cosmos is self-branching and makes a beautiful cut flower.

Growing Tips Plant seeds directly in average garden soil after danger of frost has passed, or start them indoors six weeks before transplanting. Plants may need to be

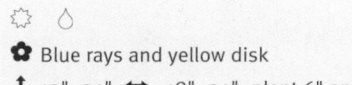

Felicia amelloides, blue marguerite.

staked as they get taller. Use fertilizer sparingly, if at all, as it promotes foliage growth at the expense of flowers. Deadhead regularly to promote season-long bloom. Cosmos frequently self-seeds.

Companion Plants The similar color of their flowers and contrasting foliage make *Cosmos* and *Cleome* excellent garden companions. *Cosmos* also mixes well with tall ornamental grasses such as feather reed grass (*Calamagrostis* × *acutiflora* 'Stricta').

Cultivars and Related Species *Cosmos bipinnatus* 'Seashell Mix' has rolled petals with an upward tilt. At just 2 feet tall, *C. bipinnatus* 'Sonata' is well suited for containers. *C. sulphureus* grows to 6 feet tall, and flowers are yellow or orange.

Felicia amelloides • Blue Marguerite

☼ ◌
✿ Blue rays and yellow disk
↕ 12"–24" ↔ 18"–24"; plant 6" apart.

The color scheme of this plant is gorgeous. Many gardeners go out of their way to combine yellow and blue flowers in their gardens, and this plant accomplishes it for you. It's a cool-weather plant and flowers best before the dog days of summer. The flowers are approximately 1½ inches wide.

Growing Tips Blue marguerite grows best in well-drained soil. Start seeds indoors and move them outside after the last frost in your area. Conscientious deadheading and fertilizing every other week will keep blue marguerite blooming. Cut it back after the first round of flowering and you'll get a second crop in early fall.

Companion Plants The flowers of *Coreopsis lanceolata* mirror the center color of the blue marguerite and make a good garden companion. Or try planting blue marguerite next to a clump of yellow bearded iris.

Cultivars and Related Species *Felicia amelloides* 'Monstrosa' has much larger flowers, which measure up to 3 inches in diameter. 'Variegata' has cream-and-green-variegated foliage.

Mauranthemum paludosum
(Leucanthemum paludosum, Chrysanthemum paludosum)

☼ ◖

✿ White rays and disk

↕ 8"–10" ↔ 12"–15"; plant 10"–12" apart.

Sometimes called mini-marguerite, this species produces masses of 1- to 1½-inch-wide flowers that look like miniature shasta daisies (*Leucanthemum × superbum*). The leaves are dark green and deeply toothed. Because the plant blooms best in cool weather, it is used as a fall and winter annual in California, the Southwest, and the deep South; in the cooler areas of these regions, it may live and bloom a second year.

Growing Tips In areas where *Mauranthemum paludosum* is grown as a winter annual, young plants are usually available in early fall, but you can also sow the seed directly into well-draining soil or in containers in October, thinning the seedlings to 10 to 12 inches apart. In cool climates, sow the seed directly in the garden in spring. This plant self-seeds.

Companion Plants *Mauranthemum paludosum* makes a great spring bulb companion, first offsetting the bulb flowers, such as tulips, later hiding the declining foliage. It works equally well with pansy (*Viola × wittrockiana*) and Iceland poppy (*Papaver nudicaule*). Or use it as a miniature temporary hedge to surround brompton stock (*Matthiola incana*).

Cultivars and Related Species *Leucanthemum multicaule* has bright yellow flowers and is lower-growing with succulentlike foliage.

Rudbeckia 'Sunset' • Black-Eyed Susan

☼ ◖

✿ Yellow, rust, orange, brown; combinations

↕ 12"–30" ↔ 12"; plant 12" apart.

You may be familiar with the perennial black-eyed susans, but there are also several annual cultivars that offer a range of warm to fiery colors. Their showy flowers are up to 9 inches in diameter and resemble those of sunflowers but are generally smaller and slightly more refined. They make excellent cut flowers.

Growing Tips Sow seeds directly in the garden or start them indoors eight to ten weeks before the last frost. Black-eyed susans grow well in average soil. They transplant easily and are heat-tolerant.

Companion Plants The foxtail plumes of *Asparagus densiflorus* 'Myersii' and the striking black leaves of *Colocasia esculenta* 'Jet Black Wonder' offer two very different types of foliage to offset *Rudbeckia* 'Sunset'.

Cultivars and Related Species The perennial *R.* 'Green Wizard' is an exotic knockout with large black center disks surrounded by green petals.

Sanvitalia procumbens
Creeping Zinnia

☼ ◖

✿ Bright yellow

↕ 6" ↔ 8"; plant 6" apart.

This little gem is perfect for the front of the border or for hiding the edges of a window box. The numerous small flowers are either single or double, about ½ inch in diameter, and are held atop slim stems and leaves, creating a delicate effect that allows you to peek through the foliage to the middle of the border.

Tagetes 'Lemon Gem', marigold.

Growing Tips Start seeds indoors or sow them directly in the garden in well-drained soil. Deadhead regularly and fertilize every two weeks to ensure constant bloom. Creeping zinnia blooms in hot and cool weather alike. It sometimes sulks for a few hours after being transplanted but will perk up quickly if watered well. To ease the shock of transplant, consider starting these seeds in individual peat pots.

Companion Plants Mix creeping zinnia with *Scaevola aemula* 'Purple Fan' at the front of a container for an outstanding color combination. Against the dark, shiny leaves of *Ajuga reptans* 'Atropurpurea' or one of the purple-leafed coral bells (*Heuchera*) the flowers of creeping zinnia really stand out.

Cultivars and Related Species *Sanvitalia procumbens* 'Sunbini' is an improved variety that has single flowers and is reported to be more floriferous.

Tagetes 'Lemon Gem', 'Tangerine Gem' • Marigolds

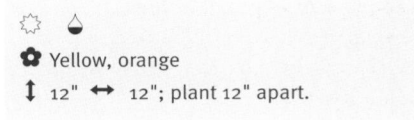

☼ 💧

✿ Yellow, orange

↕ 12" ↔ 12"; plant 12" apart.

While you may be familiar with the run-of-the-mill marigold, these two cultivars offer the sunny border or pot something more interesting. Smaller, simpler flowers (about an inch in diameter) are much more delicate than the ubiquitous pom-poms, as is the light, airy foliage. Flowers are edible and make attractive garnishes for salads, desserts, and even iced tea.

Growing Tips Sow marigold seeds in your garden two to three weeks before the last frost. They benefit from rich soil and regular fertilizing as well as deadheading.

Companion Plants As with other marigold cultivars, their insect-repellant properties make these plants useful in an herb or vegetable garden. For an attractive foliage contrast, combine them with purple-leafed basils.

Cultivars and Related Species *Tagetes patula* 'Disco Mix' is another single marigold. It grows 8 to 10 inches tall, and the yellow, orange, and red flowers are 3 inches across.

Tithonia rotundifolia
Mexican Sunflower

☼ ⬦

❀ Vermilion rays and yellow disks
↕ 4'–6' ↔ 3'–4'; plant 3' apart.

This is a tall, impressive annual. Leaves are large and covered with a velvety fuzz, and the 3- to 4-inch-wide flowers are bold and look lovely in a vase. The species is a long-season plant that blooms from late August until frost. It is heat-tolerant, endures drought and high humidity, and is rumored to be deer-resistant.

Growing Tips Start seeds indoors and move them outdoors as soon as the soil is warm. Germination takes about ten days. Mexican sunflower is not picky about soil quality.

Companion Plants For an unforgettable combination, try *Tithonia rotundifolia*

next to Persian shield (*Strobilanthes dyerianus*) or Mexican bush sage (*Salvia leucantha*). The juxtaposition of orange and purple is dynamite.

Cultivars and Related Species *Tithonia rotundifolia* 'Fiesta del Sol' is considered dwarf at 28 to 36 inches in height. 'Torch' tops out at 6 feet tall.

Zinnia angustifolia (*Z. linearis*)
Thread-Leaf Zinnia, Mexican Zinnia

☼ ⬦

❀ White or orange rays; yellow-orange disk
↕ 8"–12" ↔ 6"; plant 6" apart.

Zinnias may not be exotic, but there are very few flowers that give you more bang for your gardening buck. Thread-leaf zinnia is a single-flowered zinnia, and the simplicity of its 1½-inch flower is charming. These little guys are perfect for the front of the border; they also work well in arrangements. They are quite drought-tolerant and will bounce back from a fairly heavy wilt. Deadheading assures summer-long bloom.

Growing Tips Thread-leaf zinnia is easy to grow. Start seeds indoors six weeks before transplanting. *Zinnia angustifolia* grows well in average soil, and though plants are drought-tolerant, seedlings should not be allowed to dry out. Regular fertilizing improves flowering.

Companion Plants Thread-leaf zinnia combines well with other bright-colored annuals such as rose moss (*Portulaca grandiflora*) and many verbenas. Try clumps of them interplanted with licorice plant (*Helichrysum petiolare* 'Icicles').

Cultivars and Related Species *Zinnia angustifolia* 'Crystal White', 'Gold Star', and 'Orange Star' all have superb, clear colors. *Zinnia* 'Profusion' is slightly taller, growing 12 to 15 inches high.

Tithonia rotundifolia, **Mexican sunflower.**

Long-Lasting Flowers

What could be more satisfying than creating dried floral arrangements from the annuals you have cultivated, harvested, and dried yourself? Always harvest on dry mornings, avoiding both dew and raindrops. Tie plant stems with rubber bands into small bunches and hang them upside down. (Bunches tied with string may easily come undone as they dry, sending the flowers headfirst to the ground.) Hang the bunches in a dark, warm, well-ventilated space to dry. Occasionally check for mildew and decaying stems.

Briza maxima 'Rubra'
Red Quaking Grass

✿ Crimson-tipped spikelets

↕ 8"–24" ↔ 10"; plant 9" apart.

Originally from the Mediterranean region, this annual grass has been cultivated as a garden ornamental for nearly 200 years. Red quaking grass is loosely tufted and erect, with fairly coarse, linear leaves that are pale green fading to straw-colored in the fall. From late spring to late summer, it bears loose, open 4-inch-long panicles with 7 to 20 half-inch-long ovate heads (called spikelets), which are quite animated, dancing in the slightest breeze.

Growing Tips Sow seeds directly outdoors in early spring (which makes eradicating weed grasses a little difficult at first!), or start them indoors in well-drained soil six weeks before the last frost date. The pani-

cles are ready for harvest when the spikelets have attained full size.

Companion Plants Try a combination of quaking grass 'Rubra' with airy, cerise-pink fame flower (*Talinum calycinum*) and *Salvia splendens* 'Phoenix Bright Lilac'.

Cultivars and Related Species *Briza maxima* has spikelets tipped with reddish brown or purplish gray.

Consolida ajacis • Larkspur

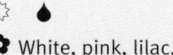

✿ White, pink, lilac, lavender, blue

↕ 12"–48" ↔ 9"–14"; plant 9"–14" apart.

Larkspur fits well into a cottage garden, old-fashioned flower bed, or cutting garden. Tall, well-branched, slender racemes of delphiniumlike spurred flowers are produced throughout the summer. Larkspur seeds are poisonous.

Growing Tips Sow seeds in the garden from early spring to early summer in light, fertile soil. Medium and tall cultivars will need support. Harvest the racemes when two thirds of the florets are open. Hang upside down in small bunches to avoid crowding and mildew.

Companion Plants Combine larkspur with *Petunia* 'Pearls Azure Blue', *Salvia* 'Cambridge Blue', and California poppy (*Eschscholzia* 'Carmine King').

Cultivars and Related Species *Consolida ajacis* 'Earl Grey' bears strong erect racemes of double slate-gray florets. The 'Dwarf Hyacinth' Series is few-branched, but the racemes are 6 to 10 inches tall, blunt-tipped, dense, and closely packed with fully double flowers. 'Frosted Skies' is 12 to 18 inches tall and displays large, semidouble mauve-lavender florets.

Gomphrena globosa
Globe Amaranth

❀ Glowing orange, purple, pink, dark blue, white, pastel shades

↕ 12"–24" ↔ 12"; plant 8" apart.

Globe amaranth is a tropical annual originally from Guatemala and Panama that's grown for its everlasting, iridescent clover-like blossoms. The plant bears its stiff, ovoid 1½-inch flower heads throughout the summer and into early autumn.

Growing Tips Sow seeds indoors six weeks before the last frost date and set them out after all danger of frost has passed. The seeds take about 15 days to germinate. Globe amaranth needs relatively fertile, well-drained soil. It is subject to powdery mildew, gray mold, and fungal leaf spots during cool, damp weather. Harvest the flowers when they are completely open but not too old. Simply gather them in bunches and hang them upside down to dry. They are easy to work with and great for children's craft projects.

Companion Plants Combine globe amaranth with *Clarkia* 'Salmon Princess' or with heat-resistant pansy *Viola* × *wittrockiana* 'Orchid Blotch' and *Petunia* 'White Swan'.

Cultivars and Related Species *Gomphrena globosa* 'Buddy' is 6 inches tall and bears deep purple flowers. 'Full Series Mixed' grows 18 to 24 inches tall and produces red, peach, pink, bright white, and orange flowers. *G. haageana,* 'Lavender Lady' offers 1½-inch round lavender flowers. 'Strawberry Fields' produces 2-inch brilliant red flowers.

Left: *Consolida ajacis,* **larkspur.**
Opposite: *Gomphrena globosa,* **globe amaranth.**

![Limonium sinuatum, statice.](full-width photograph of flowering plants)

Limonium sinuatum, statice.

Gossypium herbaceum 'Nigra'
Levant Cotton

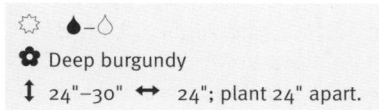

☼ ◐–◌
❀ Deep burgundy
↕ 24"–30" ↔ 24"; plant 24" apart.

An upright tender shrub, this spectacular cultivar of the commercial fiber crop bears some of the darkest foliage and stems. The walnut-size seedpods, called bolls, split open when ripe to reveal white, fluffy cotton fibers, often referred to as lint. The 3-inch-wide hibiscuslike flowers are also quite beautiful and develop with the heat of midsummer.

Growing Tips Levant cotton needs average garden soil and rarely requires staking. It relishes the heat and humidity of high summer. Start seeds indoors in individual pots four to six weeks before the last frost date. Harvest boll-bearing branches on dry, warm mornings when the seedpods are just about to burst open. You can lightly spray the thoroughly dried bolls with a fixative to prevent the fibers from dislodging.

Companion Plants Combine levant cotton with eggplant (*Solanum melongena* 'Black Enorma'), poppy (*Papaver paeoniflorum* 'Black Peony'), or *Haloragis erecta* 'Molten Bronze.'

Cultivars and Related Species *Gossypium barbadense*, sea island cotton, a native of tropical South America and the Caribbean, has several selections that produce tan, brown, or rust-colored lint.

Limonium sinuatum 'Art Shades'
Statice

☼ ◌
❀ Red, apricot, blue, yellow, white, pastel shades
↕ 16" ↔ 12"; plant 8"–12" apart.

Originally from the Mediterranean region, statice is a perennial that's typically cultivated as an annual. It is excellent for seaside gardens. From summer to early fall, winged, slightly leafy stems bear panicles of clustered spikelets that consist of tiny funnel-shaped flowers 3/8- to ½-inch long enclosed in a hairy calyx of white or pale violet.

Growing Tips Taprooted statice resents transplanting, so plant seeds directly in the garden in spring in sandy, moderately fertile, well-drained soil. Harvest mature stalks on dry mornings when the panicles are half- to two-thirds open; gather them into small bunches to avoid mildew, and hang them upside down to dry.

Companion Plants Pair statice with breadseed poppy (*Papaver somniferum* 'Double Raspberry Blush' or 'Applegreen'), *Gazania* 'Kiss Series Rose', and geranium (*Pelargonium* 'Horizon Salmon').

Cultivars and Related Species *Limonium sinuatum* 'Forever Gold' produces yellow flowers. Plants in the 'Petite Bouquet' Series are dwarf, with tightly bunched spikelets in blue, purple, deep salmon-pink, pure white, creamy white, lemon-yellow, and golden yellow.

Moluccella laevis • Bells-of-Ireland

✿ White flower within chartreuse calyx
↕ 36" ↔ 12"; plant 12" apart.

Bells-of-Ireland is an old-fashioned annual cherished for its upright 12-inch spikes that bear flowers with prominent green funnel- or bell-shaped calyces. The light green foliage is scalloped and very pretty as well. Use the flower spikes in linear or parallel designs or try them in fresh or dried wreaths or swags.

Growing Tips Bells-of-Ireland require moderately fertile, well-drained soil and may need staking if planted in a windy spot. Start the seeds six to eight weeks before the last frost date in individual 3-inch peat or newspaper pots to avoid disturbing the plant's taproot when transplanting later

on. Do not cover the seeds, as they need light to germinate. Harvest flower spikes at any stage for drying; be sure to hang them individually in order not to crush the calyces.

Companion Plants Play up the green calyces of bells-of-Ireland with chartreuse-flowered *Zinnia* 'Envy Double' or flowering tobacco (*Nicotiana langsdorffii*). Or pair it with coleus (*Solenostemon* 'Super Chartreuse').

Cultivars and Related Species None.

Proboscidea louisianica • Unicorn Plant

✿ Pale apricot-salmon speckled with darker hues; prominent yellow stamens
↕ 12" ↔ 30"; plant 30" apart.

Cultivated for its remarkable seedpods, which are about 6 inches long and reminiscent of milkweed pods except that they have two long, curling horns, unicorn plant is native to the southern United States southward to Mexico. The 2-inch, open-throated flowers look like a cross between a foxglove and a gloxinia.

Growing Tips Unicorn plants need fertile, moisture-retentive, well-drained soil. Start seeds indoors four weeks before the last frost date. Harden off the seedlings well before transplanting outdoors. Harvest when the seedpods are almost completely ripe. They will split open as they dry.

Companion Plants Try teaming unicorn plant with silvery-white and gray-leafed annuals, such as *Salvia argentea* or *Senecio cineraria* 'Silver Dust'. Pair it with bold blessed thistle (*Silybum marianum*) for an astonishing visual effect.

Cultivars and Related Species A related genus, *Martynia annua*, devil's claw, closely resembles the unicorn plant in all aspects but is more procumbent in growth habit. It is perfect to grow on fences and trellises.

Xeranthemum annuum, **immortelle**.

Scabiosa prolifera • **Carmel Daisy**

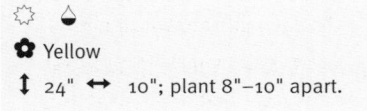

❀ Yellow

↕ 24" ↔ 10"; plant 8"–10" apart.

Native to the Mediterranean from Israel to Turkey, carmel daisy is cultivated for its profusion of 2-inch-wide, round pincushion-style inflorescences that bloom throughout the summer. When the yellow petals are shed, peachy–light green, funnel-shaped papery calyces are left behind.

Growing Tips Carmel daisies are insect- and disease-resistant and best cultivated in moderately fertile, well-drained neutral or slightly alkaline soil. Keep harvesting the flowers to ensure continuous bloom. Harvest carmel daisies on dry mornings any time after the petals have dropped. Hang to dry individually to avoid crushing or misshaping the globoid heads.

Companion Plants Combine carmel daisy with bells-of-Ireland (*Moluccella laevis*)

and Madagascar periwinkle (*Catharanthus roseus* 'Santa Fe') in front of sunflower (*Helianthus* 'Apricot Twist').

Cultivars and Related Species *Scabiosa stellata* bears round seedheads. *S. stellata* 'Drumstick' bears light blue flowers that turn to bronze, and 'Ping Pong' produces small white seedheads.

Xeranthemum annuum • **Immortelle**

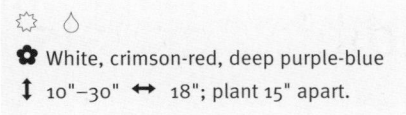

❀ White, crimson-red, deep purple-blue

↕ 10"–30" ↔ 18"; plant 15" apart.

Grown for its delicate, daisylike 2-inch flowers, which are produced all summer long, immortelle is native to southeastern Europe, the Caucusus, and Iran. The plant has an ethereal quality that plays up more robustly configured annuals. Flowers may be single or double.

Growing Tips Immortelles require well-drained, moderately fertile soil. In windy sites they may need some support. They are generally free from pests and diseases. Start seeds indoors four to six weeks before the last frost date. Keep flowers picked to ensure continuous production. For best results, harvest the flowers before they are fully open and hang them upside down in small bunches to dry.

Companion Plants Combine immortelles with pastel pink *Helichrysum macranthum* (also good for drying), toadflax (*Linaria purpurea* 'Springside White'), and soft pink, royal blue, and pure-white *Ageratum houstonianum* 'Hawaii Mixed'.

Cultivars and Related Species *Xeranthemum annuum* 'Snow Lady' produces single white flower heads. *Xeranthemum cylindraceum* 'Lilac Star' grows to about 24 inches tall and produces single mauve-pink flowers. It is also exceptional for drying.

Edible Annuals

As gardeners across the country become more plant-savvy, they are going beyond cultivating separate flower beds, herb gardens, and vegetable gardens to meld the three into an American version of the French *potager fleuri,* creating gardens that provide season-long interest for the eye as well as the palate. Here is a selection of edible plants to spice up your annual beds, borders, and pots.

Abelmoschus esculentus 'Burgundy' Purple-Leafed Okra

⊕ Ivory mallow-shaped flowers, followed by horn-shaped burgundy pods

↕ 4' in the South; 24"–36" in the North
↔ 24"–36"; plant 24"–36" apart.

Shrubby purple-leafed okra has dark green foliage with deep burgundy midribs and leaf stalks. Branches with mature pods make fine additions to fresh or dried flower arrangements. Immature pods are an integral part of gumbos and other rich soups and stews, where their mucilaginous quality (which they lose when sautéed) is appreciated.

Growing Tips Heat- and humidity-loving okra requires rich soil enhanced with rotted manure or compost. In the North, start seeds indoors four to six weeks before the last frost date and harden off seedlings before setting them out. The plants begin to bear fruit 60 days from seed.

Abelmoschus esculentus 'Burgundy', purple-leafed okra.

Companion Plants Combine purple-leafed okra with coleus (*Solenostemon* 'Night Skies' or 'Purple Emperor') and elephant ears (*Colocasia* 'Black Velvet') for a traffic-stopping display with a tropical air.

Cultivars and Related Species There are many green cultivars of okra, including 'Cajun Delight', which bears dark green, spineless pods, and 'Cowhorn', which may grow to 8 feet.

Basella alba 'Rubra'
Red-Stemmed Malabar Spinach

☼ ◐
⊕ Red stems, highly textured foliage, and attractive berries
↕ 8'–10' ↔ 8'–10'; plant 12" apart.

This vigorous fleshy-leafed vining annual is a rampant grower that requires training. Small, tight, vertical clusters of peppercorn-shaped flowers often appear late in the season. Handsome glossy black berries follow, but depending on the zone, they may or may not ripen. Leaves and young shoots are good raw in salads, or they can be steamed, braised, stir-fried, sautéed, or added to soups, stews, or curries.

Growing Tips Malabar spinach requires rich, compost-laden soil. It relishes summer's heat and humidity but does not handle drought well. Start seeds indoors six weeks before the last frost date and transplant after the soil has warmed.

Companion Plants Use Malabar spinach as a backdrop, for example, behind black cotton (*Gossypium herbaceum* 'Nigrum'), any eggplant (*Solanum melongena*), tomato (*Lycopersicon esculentum*), or hot or bell pepper (*Capsicum annuum*). Try it with *Euphorbia marginata* 'Summer Icicle', sunflower (*Helianthus* 'Claret'), or tall *Zinnia* 'Big Red Hybrid'.

Cultivars and Related Species *Basella alba* has yellow stems, which may work better for certain color schemes.

Beta vulgaris • Swiss Chard

☼ ◐
⊕ Shiny green upright foliage and colorful leaf stalks
↕ 24" ↔ 18"; plant 16" apart.

Swiss chard deserves a place in every bed, border, or container. It bears broad, slightly crinkled leaves held upright on thick, crunchy petioles (leaf stalks), both of which are edible. Eat chard braised, sautéed, steamed, or boiled; use the leaves to wrap fillings; or add them to lasagna, casseroles, or soups. Young leaves make a tasty salad green.

Growing Tips Plant chard seeds directly in friable, fertile soil in spring for summer harvest or in midsummer for harvesting in fall. Thin the seedlings to 12 inches apart and use the thinnings in salads. Chard is a cut-and-come-again vegetable—leaves that are harvested for cooking will soon be replaced with fresh foliage. Be sure to harvest chard before it flowers.

Companion Plants The vertical growth habit of chard lends itself to formal plantings in rows, as an edging plant, or in clumps throughout the garden. Plant chard with purple brussels sprouts (*Brassica oleracea* 'Falstaff') or blue-green miniature cabbage (*Brassica oleracea* 'Gonzales'). For something different, pair it with *Pentas* 'New Look Rose'.

Cultivars and Related Species *Beta vulgaris* 'Bright Lights' has petioles in light green, yellow, red, and pink. 'Rainbow' is a mix of plants with red, orange, pink, yellow, and cream petioles. 'Rhubarb' ('Ruby Red') bears large, crinkled, shiny green blades held upon stout red petioles.

Opposite: *Beta vulgaris*, Swiss chard.

Brassica oleracea var. acephala • Kale

☼ ●

⊕ Attractive foliage in blue-green, dark green, or true blue as well as white, ivory, pink, cerise, and red, which develops when the weather cools in fall

↕ 36" ↔ 36" for flowering types; plant 8"–10" apart. ↕ 12" ↔ 15"; plant 12" apart.

Edible and ornamental forms of kale are wonderful, robust, highly textured foliage plants to mix into an annual planting. The leaves are high in iron and calcium and may be served raw in salads when young and tender; older leaves are delicious steamed, braised, sautéed, or deep-fried.

Growing Tips Kale is quite hardy and may survive winters as far north as Zone 4, but it does not do well in areas warmer than Zone 8. Direct-sow seeds or set out hardened-off seedlings (started indoors six weeks before) around the last frost date,

using hot caps if required. In warmer areas, use it as a cool-season annual, sowing seed in late summer or setting out plants in fall. Kale does not require overly rich soil, but it's beneficial to apply a high-nitrogen fertilizer once.

Companion Plants Plant ornamental kale with amaranth (*Amaranthus* 'Summer Poinsettia Mix') or annual foxtail grass (*Pennisetum setaceum* 'Rubrum'). Play up the blue tones of the heirloom cultivars with chartreuse-flowered *Zinnia* 'Envy', flowering tobacco (*Nicotiana* 'Lime Green'), or light-green-leafed ornamental sweet potato (*Ipomoea batatas* 'Margarita'). As a cool-season annual, combine flowering kale with alyssum (*Lobularia maritima*), primroses (*Primula*), stock (*Matthiola longipetala*), or other pastel-flowered annuals, or use it as a mass planting for dramatic effect.

Cultivars and Related Species *Brassica oleracea* var. *acephala* 'Chou Palmier', or palm tree cabbage, an heirloom cultivar, bears spectacular narrow, recurved, savoyed (curled and wrinkled) purple-blue leaves in a rosette on top of an elongated stem. 'Coral Queen' has deep rose-red centers and finely incised foliage. 'Lacinato' has deeply cut flat leaves. 'Nagoya Mix' has lacy leaves in carmine and white.

Capsicum annuum • Hot Pepper

☼ ●

⊕ Fruits in many shapes and sizes, often changing color from green to yellow, orange, red, purple, or muted puce as they ripen

↕ 16"–48" ↔ 16"–48"; plant 12" apart.

Hot peppers are available in a wide variety of shapes, ranging in size from ½ to 4 or more inches in length. Plants simultaneously bear flowers and fruits in different stages of ripening. Many cultivars are

Brassica oleracea var. *acephala*, kale.

Capsicum annuum 'Chilly Chili', hot pepper.

listed as ornamentals, but that does not imply they are inedible—in fact, the fruits are mostly infernally hot and not for the faint-hearted. Use them fresh or dried or cut them on the branch for fresh or dried arrangements. If you have sensitive skin, wear rubber gloves when handling hot peppers.

Growing Tips Peppers require rich, fertile but well-drained soil. Grow them in the ground or in pots. Try overwintering smaller cultivars in a greenhouse, but watch out for whiteflies and aphids. Peppers are hardy in Zones 10 and 11. Sow seeds indoors six to eight weeks before the last frost date.

Companion Plants Use shorter pepper cultivars as border plants with dwarf snapdragons (*Antirrhinum* 'Double Sweetheart Mixed'), *Alyssum* 'Apricot Shades', or *Calendula* 'Apricots and Oranges' to soften the hot colors of the red-, yellow-, and orange-fruited peppers. Try the purple-fruited selections with prairie gentian (*Eustoma* 'Double Eagle Mixed') or angel's trumpet (*Brugmansia* 'Black Currant Swirl') to play up the plum and mauve shades.

Cultivars and Related Species *Capsicum annuum* 'Fatali' is 3 to 4 feet tall and bears 2- to 3-inch, wrinkled yellow habanero-style peppers. 'Filus Blue' has violet-tinged foliage speckled with white. Small ovoid upright fruit are purple for a long time before turning red. 'Little Elf' grows to 16 inches tall and wide and bears ½- to ¾-inch peppers that begin yellow tinged with purple and ripen to orange and finally red.

Manihot esculenta 'Variegata'
Variegated Cassava

☼-☼ 💧

⊕ Foliage with creamy yellow in the center of each leaflet and carmine-red leaf stalks

↕ 36"–48" ↔ 12"–36"; ↕ 12' ↔ 36"–48" in tropical areas; plant 24" apart.

Cassava, the commercial source of tapioca, is a tropical perennial native to southern Brazil and may be grown as a large shrub or small tree depending on the climate. The bark is gray to dark gray. Variegated cassava is a fabulous cultivar with spectacular palmately lobed leaves. The smooth-skinned roots may be as long as 3½ feet and are good boiled, fried, baked, and steamed. They are also ground into meal and made into ethnic breads such as bammies, fufu, and dumboy, as well as into cereal, sweetmeats, syrup, pastries, chips, and arrowroot powder.

Growing Tips Variegated cassava requires moderately fertile, well-drained soil. Grow it outdoors year-round in Zones 10 and 11, and with luck in the warmer areas of Zone 9. In colder areas, it makes a highly ornamental greenhouse plant in winter.

Companion Plants Pair variegated cassava with yellow-flowered shrub verbena (*Lantana camara*), annual sunflower (*Helianthus annuus* 'Teddy Bear'), or coleus (*Solenostemon* 'Lime Light').

Cultivars and Related Species None.

Petroselinum crispum • Parsley

☼-☼ 💧

⊕ Brilliant emerald-green, textured foliage

↕ 6"–10" ↔ 8"–12"; plant 8" apart.

Parsley makes a charming skirt for herb, vegetable, or flower gardens and is attractive in containers. Freshly harvested leaves are also an essential seasoning used in many vegetable, fish, and meat dishes, and in butters, sauces, and dressings. A good cool-season annual in the West, parsley is very hardy and will survive well into winter in the East as well.

Growing Tips Plant parsley in rich, well-drained soil. The seed can take from two to four weeks to germinate; soaking the seeds in warm water for about a day before sowing will help speed germination. Although technically a biennial that will reseed itself, parsley is best sown anew every year.

Companion Plants Parsley is a great plant to add texture to displays with larger flowering annuals such as *Mauranthemum paludosum,* pot marigold (*Calendula officinalis*), primrose (*Primula*), and pansy (*Viola* × *wittrockiana*).

Cultivars and Related Species Curly parsley, *Petroselinum crispum* var. *crispum*, has finely cut, crinkled leaves. Italian parsley, *P. crispum* var. *neapolitanum*, has much broader, flat leaves and a stronger flavor than curly parsley.

Saccharum officinarum 'Violaceum'
Purple Sugarcane

☼ 💧

⊕ Dusky purple canes

↕ 6' in the North; 10'–16' where it is hardy

↔ 3'–4'; plant 3' apart.

A cultivar of the commercial crop plant, purple sugarcane has bamboolike canes and reddish-purple leaves up to 5 feet long and up to 2½ inches wide. Use it in great clusters or as a summer screen for a tropical touch. Purple sugarcane rarely blooms in the North, but established plants cultivated in tropical areas will produce great fluffy white plumes similar to those of Pampas grass.

Growing Tips Hardy to Zones 10 and 11, sugarcane thrives in heat and humidity. It

Saccharum officinarum, purple sugarcane.

prefers compost-rich soil that's water-retentive but well-drained. Regular applications of organic fertilizers or manure teas will enhance growth. Overwinter potted plants in a greenhouse or take stem cuttings in early fall and root them indoors.

Companion Plants Because of its grand stature, purple sugarcane requires big and bold companions. Plant it with elephant ears (*Colocasia affinis* var. *jeningsii* 'Black Princess') and *Canna* 'Pink Sunburst'. Also pair it with castor bean (*Ricinus communis* 'Carmencita') and Abyssinian banana (*Ensete* 'Maurelii').

Cultivars and Related Species *Saccharum officinarum* 'California Stripe' has long green leaves variegated with a bright white stripe running along the midrib and thinner white stripes through the blades. 'Pele's Smoke' is a duskier puce-purple than 'Violaceum', with incredibly shiny purple-black canes.

Solanum melongena • Eggplant

⊕ Lavender flowers and brightly colored fruit

↕ 48" ↔ 36"; plant 18"–24" apart.

Laden with intrinsically beautiful shiny-skinned and variously hued fruit, eggplant works wonderfully well in the landscape, adding a new dimension of garden ornament. Of course, eggplant is delicious fried, baked, braised, grilled, sautéed, or cooked and puréed.

Growing Tips Eggplant requires well-drained fertile soil and appreciates recurring applications of manure or compost tea. Watch for flea beetles, and if necessary, use your favorite organic insecticide to eradicate them. In areas with heat and drought conditions, spider mite may be a problem. Eggplant is hardy to Zones 10 to 11.

Companion Plants Try the purple-skinned eggplants with *Petunia* 'Horizon Lavender' or 'Chiffon Morn' and flowering tobacco (*Nicotiana langsdorffii* or *N.* 'Havana Mixed') to complement or play up the purple hues. Combine the white, yellow, or orange-skinned eggplants with snapdragon (*Antirrhinum* 'Frosted Sunset') or angel's trumpet (*Datura* 'Double Golden Queen').

Cultivars and Related Species Heirloom *Solanum melongena* 'Antigua' bears white fruit with streaks of violet fading to soft lavender that grow to 8 inches long and 3 inches wide. 'Golden Yellow' displays bright-yellow fruit. 'Neon Hybrid' bears nearly cylindrical electric pink-purple fruit. The outstanding 'Red Egg' produces bright red ovoid fruit. 'Turkish Orange' is an heirloom that bears 3-inch, globoid fruit that turn bright orange when mature. *S. aethiopicum* 'Aubergine du Mali', is native to Mali, in western

Solanum muricatum, melon pear.

Africa, and bears flat, wrinkled and ribbed, pumpkin-shaped light green fruit that turn bright red when ripe.

Solanum muricatum
Melon Pear, Pepino

☼ ◖–◗

❀ Bright blue flowers, clusters of 5" ivory-colored fruit with lavender stripes

↕ 36" ↔ 36"; plant 24"–36" apart.

Native to the Andes, melon pear is an excellent addition to the flower border or pot. The foliage is fairly rough and as long as 6 inches. The fruit is highly ornamental and has a fine melon flavor and fragrance. Eat fresh melon pear chilled, scooping the flesh out of the skin with a spoon.

Growing Tips Melon pear requires a sheltered spot with well-drained, fertile soil. It responds well to applications of com-

post. It needs a long growing season to ripen the fruit thoroughly, and northern gardeners may have to bring the plant indoors to complete the process. Thinning will produce larger, better-shaped fruit. Overwinter containerized plants in a sunny greenhouse. Watch for whiteflies and spider mites indoors. A tender perennial, melon pear is hardy to Zones 10 and 11.

Companion Plants Use melon pear with star thistle (*Centaurea* 'Black Ball'), Lavatera 'Loveliness Mixed', or *Clarkia* 'Lady in Blue' to play up the lavender stripes on the fruit.

Cultivars and Related Species *Solanum muricatum* 'Cascade Gold' bears heart-shaped fruit with golden skin striped with purple. 'Miski Prolific' produces creamy white fruit with a faint salmon glow and light purple stripes, and 'Toma' has cream-colored fruit striped with dark purple.

Annuals With Fabulous Foliage

Not all of the fabulous plants cultivated as annuals are grown for their flowers. Many are selected because of leaf texture, color, size, or their attractive growth habit. Foliage with fascinating shapes, interesting spines or hairs, or captivating colors adds new visual intrigue and distinctive architectural aspects to beds, borders, window boxes, and container plantings. The cut foliage adds a new dimension to fresh flower arrangements. In their native habitats, many of the plants in this section are considered herbaceous perennials or even shrubs.

Breynia nivosa 'Roseopicta'
Snowbush

☼ ◔-◐

⊕ Delicate foliage marbled with green, white, and rosy-pink supported by wiry maroon-colored stems

↕ 36"; ↔ 24"–36"; plant 24" apart.

Native to the South Pacific, snowbush, a slender, delicate evergreen shrub with highly variegated foliage and colorful stems, makes a pretty summer accent plant for shaded areas or container plantings. Cut branches work well in fresh flower arrangements. Snowbush rarely blooms in the summer border.

Growing Tips Snowbush requires rich, compost-enhanced soil and will defoliate if allowed to dry out. Keep the plant pinched to encourage a bushy appearance. Although it prefers rather high humidity, snowbush can be overwintered indoors in a warm greenhouse or on a windowsill that receives filtered sunlight. Or take soft-wood cuttings in summer. Spider mites, whiteflies, and aphids are often meddlesome indoors. Hardy to Zones 10 to 11.

Companion Plants Use snowbush with such summer bulbs as *Caladium* and *Achimenes* or annuals such as *Torenia* 'Happy Faces Mixed', *Browallia speciosa* 'Silver Bells', and *Impatiens* 'Passion Seashells'.

Cultivars and Related Species None.

Cissus discolor • Rex-Begonia Vine

☼-☼ ◐

⊕ Two-toned leaves: topsides patterned with silver and gray or pink stripes; maroon undersides

↕ 6'–10'; ↔ 10"; plant 8" apart.

This familiar vining houseplant gives height and spectacular color to the shady garden or window box. Rex-begonia vine rarely blooms as a summer annual, but in warmer areas or in a greenhouse in colder

Cissus discolor, rex-begonia vine.

climates it may produce small 2½-inch panicles of red-tinted green flowers, followed by clusters of ⅜-inch, deep red berries.

Growing Tips Rex-begonia vine needs compost-rich, moisture retentive well-drained soil. This tropical vine scrambles upward by means of coiling red tendrils and needs plant supports or a fence to climb on. Spider mites, mealy bugs, and whiteflies can be a problem in the greenhouse or outdoors in tropical zones. *Cissus discolor* is hardy to Zones 10 and 11.

Companion Plants Use rex-begonia vine as a backdrop for any number of ornamental begonia species and cultivars, including rex begonias and *Begonia* 'Silver Queen'. Additionally, team it up with *Hypoestes* 'Confetti Red' or 'Confetti White'.

Cultivars and Related Species None.

Cynara scolymus • Globe Artichoke

● 20" pinnately divided, silver-gray spiny leaves

↕ 5' ↔ 4'; plant 3'–4' apart.

The globe artichoke, a clump-forming thistle relative from the southwestern Mediterranean, makes a bold addition to the annual bed. It attains a height of 4 to 5 feet and a width of 6 feet. It is hardy to Zones 8 to 9 but does best in areas with cool foggy summers. (It is grown commercially in the Monterey Bay area of California.) New plants are easy to start by dividing the root ball.

Growing Tips Start seeds indoors six to eight weeks before the last frost date. They will germinate in ten days or more. Once they have germinated, keep the seedlings at 65°F to 70°F for about six weeks. Ideally, night temperatures should dip to about 60°F. Once the first set of true leaves are 3 inches long, transplant the seedlings to individual pots. Then place them in an environment where temperatures never climb above 50°F for about two weeks. As soon as the soil is at least 50°F, plant the artichokes in the garden.

Companion Plants Globe artichoke is a big, bold architectural plant that requires grand neighbors. For example, plant it with 5-foot-tall annual sunflower (*Helianthus annuus* 'Valentine' or 'Pastiche') or variegated corn (*Zea mays* 'Quadricolor'). Alternatively, pair it with your favorite 4- or 5-foot-tall dahlia cultivars.

Cultivars and Related Species *Cynara scolymus* 'Green Globe' has been popular for years. 'Imperial Star' is a hybrid that is claimed to produce more artichokes than 'Green Globe'.

Euphorbia marginata, **snow-on-the-mountain.**

Euphorbia marginata
Snow-on-the-Mountain

☼–☼ ◊

● 3" ovate, medium green leaves with white variegation or margins

↕ 12"–36" ↔ 12"; plant 12" apart.

This old-fashioned annual poinsettia relative is native to the southwestern United States and Mexico. It initially grows as a single stem but later branches extensively. Its milky latex may cause dermatitis in sensitive individuals. From late summer to early autumn, it produces terminal umbels of green-white flowers and involucres, both variegated, margined, or spotted white up to 12 inches across. They make excellent long-lasting cut flowers.

Growing Tips Snow-on-the-mountain resents transplanting; therefore sow seeds directly in the garden in spring. This plant will volunteer readily in many areas. It tolerates poor soil, heat, drought, and partial shade but will grow larger in light, freely draining, moderately fertile soil in a sunny site.

Companion Plants Combine snow-on-the-mountain with *Osteospermum* 'Pastel Silks', *Cosmos* 'Purity', and marigold (*Tagetes* 'Sweet Cream') for an all white, drought-resistant design.

Cultivars and Related Species *Euphorbia marginata* 'Summer Icicle' is comparatively dwarf at 18 inches tall. *Euphorbia heterophylla,* the annual poinsettia, grows 2 to 2½ feet tall and bears a distinct resemblance to *E. pulcherrima.* It too withstands poor soils, heat, and drought and colors up by midsummer. It is good for picking, as well.

Melianthus major · Honey Flower

☼ ◐

⊕ 12" to 20", alternate, pinnate gray-green foliage with 9 to 17 stridently toothed leaflets

↕ 3'–4' ↔ 3'–4' in a season;
↕ 10' ↔ 10' in tropical zones; plant 3' apart.

Once obscure in cultivation, this South African shrub has taken the gardening world by storm as an annual. It is a robust plant with hollow stems and predominant stipules that lends a tropical air to beds, borders, and containers. Honey flower rarely blooms if grown as an annual.

Growing Tips Grow honey flower in moderately fertile, moisture-retentive but well-drained soil. Start seeds indoors in spring. Root softwood cuttings in late spring or early summer. Overwinter it indoors in a cool, sunny greenhouse or garden room. Water less in winter. Watch for spider mites and whiteflies. Hardy to Zones 8 to 11.

Companion Plants Combine honey flower with any of your favorite dark-leaved *Canna* cultivars, such as 'Pink Sunburst'

or 'Prince Charmant', along with the spectacular banana *Musa* 'Variegated Hawaiian'.

Cultivars and Related Species *Melianthus comosus* and *M. villosus* are less commonly cultivated.

Oryza sativa 'Nigrescens' Purple-Leafed Rice

☼ ◐–◐◐

⊕ Loosely arching, broadly linear, 3' dark brownish-purple leaves.

↕ 30" ↔ 12"; plant 10" apart.

This ornamental selection of the commercial crop plant is a most intriguing annual grass. From midsummer to mid-autumn it produces spikelets in open arching panicles up to 14 inches long. Purple-leafed rice makes an unusual addition to a water garden, especially when combined with broad-leafed aquatic plants. In addition to attracting seed-eating birds and wildlife, the dark brownish-purple flower panicles look lovely in fresh or dried arrangements.

Growing Tips Cultivate purple-leafed rice in fertile, clay-loam soil or alternately, use it as a marginal pond plant in pots at the water's edge or in a containerized water garden. It needs a minimum temperature of 50°F in order to succeed. Surface-sow the seeds at 66°F to 75°F in late winter in clay pots standing in water when soil is thoroughly warmed.

Companion Plants Play up the dark hues of purple-leafed rice by pairing it with variegated bog or marginal plants such as *Iris pseudacorus* 'Variegata', sweet flag (*Acorus calamus* 'Variegatus'), or the variously toned *Houttynia cordata* 'Chameleon'.

Cultivars and Related Species *Oryza sativa* 'Red Dragon' has redder foliage than 'Nigrescens'.

Melianthus major, honey flower.

Ricinus communis, castor bean.

Ricinus communis • Castor Bean

☼ ◗

⊕ 6" to 18" glossy, palmately lobed medium green, reddish-purple, or bronzy-red leaves; softly spiny seed capsules

↕ 6' ↔ 3' in a season; ↕ 30' ↔ 12' in tropical areas; plant 3'–4' apart.

An erect, branching, fast-growing mound-forming shrub indigenous to North Africa and the Middle East, castor bean is commonly cultivated as an annual. All plant parts, especially the seeds, are toxic and contact with the foliage may cause dermatitis in people with sensitive skin. The mature seeds are the source for castor oil.

Growing Tips Castor bean requires fertile, humus-rich, moisture-retentive but well-drained soil. Soak seeds for 24 hours and sow them indoors in 3-inch pots six weeks before the last frost date. Or sow them directly in the garden when the soil is thoroughly warmed. Castor beans resent transplanting. They may need staking in windy sites.

Companion Plants Combine castor bean with other large-scale bold tropical plants like red-striped banana (*Musa acuminata* subsp. *sumatrana*, or 'Rojo'), Abyssinian banana (*Ensete* 'Maurelii'), or *Canna* 'Pink Sunburst', which has pink-striped maroon leaves.

Cultivars and Related Species *Ricinus communis* 'Carmencita' is well branched and reaches 6 to 10 feet; it bears dark bronze-red foliage and bright red flowers. 'Impala' is compact at 4 feet and displays reddish-purple foliage and yellowish-green flowers. 'Red Spire' grows to 6 to 10 feet and carries bronze-flushed foliage.

Solanum atropurpureum

☼ ◗

⊕ Deep purple stems, leaf petioles, sharp thorns and clusters of round white fruit ripening to yellow, then brilliant orange

↕ 4' ↔ 3'; plant 3' apart.

At first sight this Brazilian native looks like a monstrous hybrid of an eggplant and a cactus, but it is a wildly interesting small shrub often cultivated as an annual. The glossy green foliage is about 6 inches long, ovate, and deeply lobed. This plant makes a spectacular specimen either in a pot or in the garden. It is also effective as an annual hedge to deter dogs or other unwanted visitors.

Growing Tips *Solanum atropurpureum* requires fertile, moisture-retentive but well-drained soil. Start seeds indoors six or eight weeks before the last frost date and set out hardened-off plantlets when the soil is thoroughly warmed. Plants can be overwintered in a temperate greenhouse. Hardy to Zones 10 and 11.

Companion Plants Play up architectural *Solanum atropurpureum* with other equally bold tropical plants such as red-leaf ginger (*Hedychium greenii*) or variegated New Zealand flax (*Phormium* 'Aurora'), which has long, striped leaves.

Cultivars and Related Species None are commonly available.

Evening Bloomers

If you're someone who enjoys relaxing in the garden at night, sipping a cool beverage after a long day's work, evening bloomers may be among your favorite garden companions. The plants described here are fragrant and in full bloom at night, adding scent and color to your garden after hours.

Datura inoxia • Angel's Trumpet

☼ ◆

❀ White, pink, lavender; white tinged with pink or lavender

↕ 36" ↔ 24"; plant 24" apart.

Angel's trumpet is best appreciated at dusk, when the large white blooms fairly glow in the fading light. Blossoms are held upright and can be 6 to 8 inches in length. The plant does equally well in a container or border.

Growing Tips Angel's trumpet starts easily from seed but grows slowly; it can take nine months from seed to bloom. Angel's trumpet likes it hot, so don't plant it outdoors until several weeks after the danger of frost has passed. It grows in ordinary soil but will thrive in moist, rich soil. Fertilize every other week and keep an eye out for spider mites. Take cuttings in late summer to expand your collection for the following spring.

Companion Plants Try combining angel's trumpet with shorter plants that echo the flower color: Twinspur (*Diascia barberae*)

Datura inoxia, angel's trumpet.

comes in several shades of pink that nicely complement the pink angel's trumpet, and *Scaevola aemula* highlights purple-tinged trumpets. If you grow white angel's trumpet, choose a plant with wild-colored foliage to surround it, like parrot leaf (*Alternanthera ficoidea*). *Datura* will overwinter in regions that experience only light frosts.

Cultivars and Related Species *Datura metel* is similar to *D. inoxia* in growth habit but is slightly larger. Flowers open during the day and can be white, lavender, or yellow.

Ipomoea alba • Moonflower

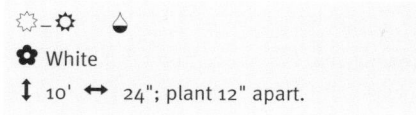

☀ White

↕ 10' ↔ 24"; plant 12" apart.

While almost everyone knows morning glory (*Ipomoea purpurea*), its nocturnal cousin, moonflower, remains a mystery to many gardeners. Trumpet-shaped flowers, 6 inches wide at the mouth, are wonderfully fragrant in the evening and closed tight during the day. This plant performs well on a trellis or railing.

Growing Tips Like many other members of its genus, moonflower flourishes in poor soils. Rich soil or frequent fertilizer applications will produce lush foliage at the expense of flowers. Moonflower is easy to start from seed, as are most of the plants in this genus. To speed things along, nick the hard seed coat or soak the seeds in warm water for eight hours before planting. Cold temperatures weaken the plant, so don't move it outdoors until the weather has warmed up. Start seed indoors six weeks before the last frost in your area. Planting seeds in individual peat pots will minimize transplant trauma.

Companion Plants As moonflower doesn't show off during the day, try planting it with companions that do. Intertwine it with hyacinth bean (*Lablab purpureus*) or with its day-blooming cousin, morning glory (*Ipomoea purpurea*).

Cultivars and Related Species Cypress vine, *Ipomoea quamoclit*, has finely cut foliage and small red flowers. It's a very fast grower, capable of covering 20 feet in a single season.

Lagenaria siceraria, gourd vine.

Lagenaria siceraria
Gourd Vine, Calabash Vine

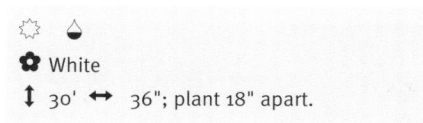

☀ White

↕ 30' ↔ 36"; plant 18" apart.

Perfuming the garden with a musky scent, the flowers of gourd vine open at night and wilt by midday. This fast-growing climber needs the support of a solid arbor or fence where it can display its showy flowers and large hanging fruits at the same time. (Native Americans used the gourds as storage containers and water vessels.)

Growing Tips Gourd vine thrives in high heat and humidity. If you grow this plant for the gourds, start seeds indoors early, at least six weeks before the last frost in your area; you'll need a long growing season. Gourd vine can be finicky about transplanting, so consider starting plants in individual peat pots.

Companion Plants The foliage of gourd vine isn't beautiful, so compensate by planting it alongside another fast-growing vine like one of the passion flowers (*Passiflora*) or bag flower (*Clerodendrum thomsonae*).

Cultivars and Related Species *Luffa cylindrica* is another vine in the cucumber family with interesting yellow flowers and fruit, whose skeleton gives us the bath loofah. Cultural requirements are similar to those of gourd vine.

Matthiola longipetala
Night-Scented Stock, Evening Stock

☼ ◗

✿ Purple, pink, white
↕ 18" ↔ 18"; plant 12" apart.

In general, multibranched night-scented stock prefers cooler temperatures. In fact, it is one of the most cold-resistant annuals available. Flowers are scattered over the top of the plant, giving it a colorful,

mounded appearance. Blooms are extremely fragrant in the evening. Stems and flowers may wilt during the heat of the day. They should revive in the evening. Night-scented stock is a good plant for attracting butterflies and other pollinating insects to your garden. It's commonly used as a winter annual in the low desert in California and Arizona.

Growing Tips Night-scented stock is easy to grow and blooms early in the year. Sow seeds thickly outdoors in early spring in moderately rich well-drained soil. Don't thin the plants as they grow; crowding speeds bloom. Or start them indoors and transplant them at the bud stage. Seeds require light for germination. In warmer areas, set out young plants in early fall for winter or early spring bloom.

Companion Plants Try planting evening stock in front of a variegated ornamental grass to offset its flowers in evening light. Reed canary grass (*Phalaris arundinacea picta*) and creeping soft grass (*Holcus mollis* 'Albovariegatus') are two worth considering.

Cultivars and Related Species *Matthiola incana* is a fragrant day bloomer with flowers held in heavily clustered terminal racemes. It can reach 30 inches tall. *Mathiola longipetala* 'Starlight Sensation' is a multicolored night bloomer. Flowers are pink and purple with white centers.

Mirabilis jalapa • Four-o'-Clock

☼-☀ ◗

✿ Red, pink, yellow, white, and striped
↕ 24"–36" ↔ 24"–36"; plant 24" apart.

As their common name suggests, four-o'-clocks open late in the day. Flowers are approximately 1 inch wide and 1 to 2

***Matthiola longipetala*, night-scented stock.**

Mirabilis jalapa 'Kaleidoscope', four-o'-clock.

inches long. There are numerous cultivars available, including dwarf varieties and some with variegated foliage. Four-o'-clocks are tough plants that can tolerate some city grime, so this is an excellent choice for urban gardeners. Gardeners in more rural areas should note that four-o'-clocks are rarely grazed by deer.

Growing Tips Four-o'-clocks grow best in well-drained average garden soil. Start seeds of this easy-to-grow annual indoors and transplant seedlings after the last frost. Dig the roots in fall and store them in a cool spot over the winter, much like *Dahlia* tubers.

Companion Plants The foliage of four-o'-clocks is not particularly noteworthy, so try surrounding them with a beautiful foliage plant, such as variegated *Iris*. If you usually enjoy your garden at night, combine four-o'-clocks with any plant with light-colored variegation in the leaves to create visual interest in dim light.

Cultivars and Related Species *Mirabilis jalapa* 'Broken Colors' sports multicolored and patterned flowers. On a single plant you can find flowers that are part yellow and part orange next to white blooms streaked with pink.

Nicotiana alata • Flowering Tobacco

☼ ⬥

❀ White, pink, red, lime-green

↕ 3'–5' ↔ 12"; plant 12" apart.

A wonderful shade annual, flowering tobacco has neat rosettes of foliage and stalks of flowers in several colors. All varieties are fragrant at night, but the white and lime-green species look most vivid in the evening garden. The plant is covered with short, sticky hairs and its juice has narcotic properties. Both of these characteristics make it an unappealing snack to wildlife—a big plus in rural areas.

Growing Tips Start easy-to-grow flowering tobacco from seed indoor six to eight weeks before the last frost date and transplant after danger of frost has passed.

Nicotiana alata, **flowering tobacco.**

Water generously during the hottest days of summer. This plant will grow in average soil but prefers slightly alkaline soil; conditioning the soil with a little lime and potash is a good idea.

Companion Plants Pair flowering tobacco with other species that share its needs: You might plant it next to your favorite *Clematis,* which also likes a slightly alkaline pH.

Cultivars and Related Species *Nicotiana sylvestris* can reach 6 feet in height and is an excellent addition to the back of the border. Flowers are tubular, white, very fragrant, and will self-seed except in very cold climates. *Nicotiana langsdorffii* (see page 59) is similar to *N. sylvestris,* but has pale green flowers. *Nicotiana × sanderae* is a dwarf plant reaching 10 inches tall.

Nymphaea lotus • Egyptian Water-Lily

☼–☼ Standing water
✿ White petals with yellow centers
↕ Flowers are held 6"–10" above leaves, which float on the water's surface; leaves are 6"–12" in diameter; plant 18" apart.

If you're lucky enough to have a water garden, try growing a tropical water-lily as an annual. There are numerous varieties to choose from, including several that open at night. The blossoms of Egyptian water-lily are closed tight during the day and open in the evening to emit an enticing scent.

Growing Tips Egyptian water-lily needs water at least 18 inches deep. Plant a single mature tuber in a large container with drainage holes. Leave the growing tip visible and cover the soil with gravel to keep tuber and soil in place. Fertilize with aquatic plant food once a month during the growing season. Where winters get too cold, use a water heater to grow tropical water-lilies year-round or dig up the tubers when water temperatures drop below 70°F and overwinter them. The tubers of tropical water-lilies look like

Nymphaea lotus **'Red Flare', Egyptian water-lily.**

walnuts and form numerous small tubers much as daffodil bulbs form bulblets. Separate these from the original tuber and pot them up individually.

Companion Plants Papyrus (*Cyperus papyrus*) is a striking aquatic plant that brings height and feathery foliage to your water garden. Make it a centerpiece and surround it with different water-lily cultivars. Plant a day-blooming water-lily alongside the evening bloomer to have bloom in your water garden around the clock.

Cultivars and Related Species *Nymphaea* 'Red Flare' is another night bloomer with dark reddish leaves and ruby-red flowers; *N.* 'Sir Galahad' has white flowers with a soft matte finish that open in the evening. *Nymphaea caerulea* is a day-blooming water-lily with a lovely pale blue flower.

Silene nutans • Catchfly

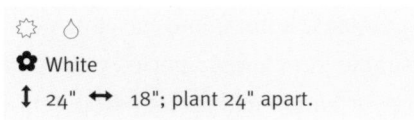

❁ White
↕ 24" ↔ 18"; plant 24" apart.

This plant is native to rocky coastal areas and grows easily in dry, poor soils. Numerous flowers are borne on slim stalks and produce a powerfully sweet smell at night. An evening breeze makes these delicate blossoms sway and releases their perfume. The common name catchfly comes from the sticky stems and calyx of the plant, which can trap small insects with its adhesive.

Growing Tips Catchfly is a warm-weather plant and shouldn't be moved outdoors until temperatures climb above 60°F. Catchfly can be fussy about transplanting, so either sow seeds where the plant will grow or start them in individual peat pots that can be transplanted straight into the garden.

Companion Plants The silvery-purple leaves of Persian shield (*Strobilanthes dyerianus*) make an excellent backdrop to set off the white flowers of catchfly. *Canna × generalis* 'Phaison', with its bronze and pink stripes, also makes for a dramatic contrast with catchfly.

Cultivars and Related Species Sweet William(*Silene armeria*) a popular rock-garden plant with pink flowers, is also valued for its scent, which is most noticeable during the day.

Zaluzianskya capensis • Night Phlox

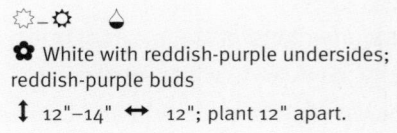

❁ White with reddish-purple undersides; reddish-purple buds
↕ 12"–14" ↔ 12"; plant 12" apart.

Night phlox is a superbly beautiful plant. Each petal is split into a V-shape, giving the flower a pinwheel look. Night phlox foliage is quite glossy. Its scent has been described as lemony, almond, or honey-like; in other words, it's pleasant. Grow this plant for its bloom and fragrance.

Growing Tips Night phlox is easy to grow from seed and should be planted outdoors after the last frost. This annual will grow in most soils and benefits from regular fertilizer applications.

Companion Plants During the day, the closed red buds of night phlox are nicely highlighted by the silvery foliage of wormwood (*Artemisia ludoviciana* 'Silver King'), which also stands out in the evening garden.

Cultivars and Related Species *Zaluzianskya capensis* 'Midnight Candy' is one of the most readily available cultivars of this rare plant. *Zaluzianskya rubrostellata* has yellow flowers with a red star in the center.

Morning Glories and Their Relatives

Some members of the morning glory clan are so similar in appearance as to be easily confused, while others are quite distinctive—from the woolly-leafed, drought-resistant silverbush (*Convolvulus cneorum*) to the creeping tropical sweet-potato vine (*Ipomoea batatas*), with lush, brightly colored leaves, to the astonishing woolly morning glory (*Argyreia nervosa*), which can twine to 30 feet tall in one season. Make the most of these exuberant, fast-growing vines from warm climates: Use them to cover trellises, pergolas, arbors, and gazebos or to hide unattractive outbuildings or other undesirable structures. Species grown for their flowers usually bloom from summer to fall or until temperatures drop below 50°F.; in warmer areas they keep going throughout the year. If you like, surround the bases of the vigorous climbers with shorter annuals in harmonizing or contrasting colors. Just be sure to leave plenty of space for air circulation between the vines and their companions.

Growing Tips

Unless otherwise specified, grow morning glories in moderately fertile, well-drained soil. Nick each seed with a file before soaking in warm water for a day or overnight. Sow seeds indoors six to eight weeks before the last frost date in individual three-inch pots to avoid disturbing the roots when you transplant the seedlings. Alternately, sow seeds in the garden after all danger of frost has passed. Supply support for the seedlings of the climbing varieties right away. If you grow morning glories in a pot, supply a balanced liquid fertilizer monthly.

Convolvulus cneorum, **silverbush**.

Argyreia nervosa
Woolly Morning Glory

✿ Lavender-blue with darker base and flushed with red-purple inside

↕ 25'–30' ↔ 5'; plant 5' apart.

This amazing morning glory relative, a native of Assam, India, and Bangladesh, is a twining liana grown for its handsome white downy young shoots and broadly ovate, silver-backed furry leaves, which are 7 to 11 inches long with heart-shaped bases. It bears axillary cymes to 6 inches long of white-down-covered buds that open into funnel-shaped flowers 2½ to 3 inches long, which are followed by attractive brown berries.

Growing Tips See page 42, above. This vine needs a very sturdy support.

Companion Plants A grand plant like woolly morning glory is best grown as a specimen, not mixed with other vines.

However it would make a bold climbing backdrop for large-scale silver plants such as globe artichoke (_Cynara scolymus_).

Cultivars None.

Convolvulus cneorum • Silverbush

✿ White with yellow centers

↕ 24" ↔ 36"; plant 18" apart.

A native of the central and western region of the Mediterranean, silverbush is a mounded bushy shrub employed as an annual. It bears inversely lance-shaped silver-green leaves from 1¼ to 2½ inches long. From late spring to summer it produces 1½-inch-wide funnel-shaped flowers in axillary clusters. This is a good choice for a drought-resistant garden. Use it in rooftop and terrace container plantings or in a pedestrian island or similar spot where delivering water may be a problem.

Convolvulus tricolor 'Royal Ensign', dwarf morning glory.

Growing Tips See page 42, above. Overwinter potted silverbush in a sunny, cold greenhouse. It is hardy to Zones 8 to 10, but resents high humidity in summer and soggy soil in winter.

Companion Plants Combine silverbush with geranium (*Pelargonium* 'White Orbit'), silver-leafed *Salvia argentea*, white-flowered mealycup sage (*Salvia farinacea* 'Silver White'), and *Zinnia angustifolia* 'Crystal White'.

Cultivars None (yet).

Convolvulus tricolor
Dwarf Morning Glory

☼ ◗
✿ Royal blue, feathered white in the throats with yellow eyes
↕ 12"–16" ↔ 9"–12"; plant 8"–10" apart.

From the warm regions of Portugal, Greece, and North Africa comes another species in the family: a bushy, upright then spreading red-stemmed annual with ovate to lance-shaped dark green leaves to 1½

inches long. Throughout the summer it produces solitary open, funnel-shaped 1½-inch-wide flowers. Each blossom lasts a single day. It makes a grand groundcover or edging plant. Alternatively, use it in a planter, where it can happily trail over the edge.

Growing Tips Definitely a labor of love, deadheading will encourage continual flower production. Hardy to Zones 9 to 10. For more tips, see page 42.

Companion Plants For a cheery mixture, team up *Convolvulus tricolor* 'Ensign Mixed' with crimson-red, 30-inch-tall *Cosmos* 'Pied Piper Red', *Penstemon heterophyllus* 'True Blue', and *Trachymene* 'Mixed Colors', which combines pink, white, and blue.

Cultivars *Convolvulus tricolor* 'Ensign Mixed' bears bi- and tri-color blossoms in shades of pink, rose, cerise, blue, and white, all with yellow throats. 'Royal Ensign' grows to 12 inches tall and produces deep blue flowers to 2 inches across.

Evolvulus pilosus

☼ ◌ ○

✿ Lavender-pink or blue

↕ 20" ↔ 20"; plant 15" apart.

From Montana, South Dakota, Arizona, and Texas comes the relatively recently introduced *Evolvulus pilosus*, which has not yet been given a common name. It is a slender, trailing evergreen subshrub most often grown as an annual. It has spoon-shaped reversed-lance-shaped, densely silky-hairy silver-gray leaves up to ½ inch long. It bears solitary short-tubed, funnel- to bell-shaped flowers ½ to ¾ inch across. This is a terrific plant to use for a pot in a sunny, hot, dry spot, or in any location that bakes in the sun and lacks water.

Growing Tips Work turkey grit or sharp sand into water-retentive soil for extra drainage. *Evolvulus pilosus* is hardy to Zone 7, but heavy, wet winter soil usually gets the better of it. For more growing tips, see page 42.

Companion Plants This is a great annual to combine with blue-flowered *Salvia chamaedryoides*, rosemary (*Rosmarinus* 'Logee's Blue'), lavender (*Lavandula stoechys*), and *Osteospermum* 'Blue Streak' for a low-maintenance, disease-resistant, rooftop or terrace container planting.

Cultivars *Evolvulus pilosus* 'Blue Daze' has elliptic-ovate, white-hairy leaves and powder-blue flowers with white eyes.

Ipomoea batatas • Sweet-Potato Vine

☼ ◌ ○

◑ Foliage multicolored or in various shades of purple-black, reddish-bronze, and chartreuse

↕ 6"; 7"–10" in warmer areas
↔ 20'; plant 12" apart.

Ornamental-leafed selections of the agricultural sweet potato, a native of tropical South America, have heart-shaped or three- to five-lobed entire leaves. Sweet-potato vines have no means of climbing; instead they clamber along the ground. Use them in great sweeps in an annual bed or let them scramble over the edges of containers. They rarely bloom. In the tropics, sweet potatoes are grown for their very sweet tasting tubers.

Growing Tips Set out young plants or rooted cuttings after all danger of frost has passed and the soil is thoroughly warmed in moderately fertile, well-drained soil in a sheltered spot. Manage sweet-potato vine rigorously, as it can easily get the better of its neighbors. Dig tubers in fall and overwinter them in peat moss. To prevent the spread of the destructive sweet potato weevil, ornamental sweet potatoes are prohibited from sale (or are about to be) in regions where sweet potatoes are grown as a commercial crop. *Ipomoea batatas* is hardy to Zones 9 to 11.

Evolvulus pilosus **'Blue Daze'.**

Ipomoea lobata, Spanish flag.

Companion Plants With so many color choices of sweet-potato vine, gardeners can go to town with plant combinations. Mix or match them with your favorite verbenas, coleus (*Solenostemon scutellarioides*), snapdragons (*Antirrhinum*), dahlias, clarkias, cannas, petunias, salvias, or chards (*Beta vulgaris*).

Cultivars and Related Species *Ipomoea batatas* 'Blackie' sports rich purple-black foliage with deeply lobed leaves. 'Ladyfingers' has three-pointed, olive-green leaves with deep purple veins. 'Margarita' ('Marguerite') bears bright chartreuse hearts that never scorch in intense sun. The leaves of 'Pink Frost' ('Tricolor') are a combination of baby pink, soft green, and creamy white. 'Margarita' and 'Pink Frost' will keep their colors in light shade.

Ipomoea lobata • Spanish Flag

☼ ◔

✿ Scarlet flowers maturing to orange through yellow and finally white

↕ 6"–12" ↔ 15"; plant 8"–12" apart.

This perennial climber grown as an annual is native to Mexico southward to Central and South America. It bears crimson-flushed stems and stalks. The 4-inch-long, medium to deep green leaves have three prominent fingerlike lobes with two to four smaller, basal ones. Dense, one-sided panicles up to 12 inches long bear slightly curved, narrow tubular ½- to ¾-inch-long flowers. The flowers are much sought after by hummingbirds and butterflies.

Growing Tips See page 42.

Companion Plants Grow Spanish flag as a specimen, planted alone to cover a lamppost or trellis. Use it as a colorful screen to back up 17-inch, bright orange dwarf sunflower (*Helianthus* 'Sundance Kid'), dwarf Mexican sunflower (*Tithonia* 'Fiesta del Sol'), and *Salvia coccinea* 'Lady in Red'.

Cultivars None.

Ipomoea × multifida
Cardinal Climber

☼ ◌

❀ Crimson-red with white throat

↕ 3'–6' ↔ 12"–15"; plant 8"–12" apart.

A hybrid of garden origin between *Ipomea coccinea,* the scarlet-flowered red morning glory from the southeastern United States, and *I. quamoclit,* the scarlet-tubed star glory, indigenous to tropical South America, cardinal climber is a slender twining annual vine with three- to seven-lobed broadly triangular-ovate medium green leaves 1½ to 5 inches long. Its 1-inch-wide, salverform (joined petals that are long and tube-shaped with a spreading upper part) flowers are quite attractive to hummingbirds and butterflies.

Growing Tips See page 42.

Companion Plants Cardinal climber is best appreciated as a specimen vine cover.

Related Species *Ipomoea quamoclit* has extremely feathery 3-inch foliage that is far finer in texture than that of cardinal climber. Their scarlet flowers are far more tube-shaped as well. Depending on the cultural conditions and zone, it can grow as much as 20 feet tall.

Ipomoea nil • Morning Glory

☼ ◌

❀ White tubes with pale to deep blue, sometimes purple or red-purple petal lobes

↕ 15' ↔ 12"–18"; plant 8"–12" apart.

This pantropical species is another relative commonly called morning glory. It is a vigorous annual (or in tropical climates, a woody-based short-lived perennial) climber with bristly yellow-haired stems. The medium green leaves are 2 to 5½ inches long and broadly ovate and sometimes three-lobed. It produces funnel-shaped flowers up to 2 inches wide.

Growing Tips See page 42.

Companion Plants Train cultivars of *Ipomoea nil* onto an obelisk or teepee in a container with light blue *Lobelia* 'Riviera Blue Splash' and white-flowered 'Regatta White', and let *Petunia* 'Double Cascade Plum Vein' creep over the edge of the pot.

Cultivars and Related Species *Ipomoea nil* 'Chocolate' bears 3-inch-wide reddish-chocolate flowers. 'Early Call' produces white-tubed flowers with scarlet lobes up to 3 inches across. The Platycodon Series has single and semidouble flowers in red, purple, or white. 'Scarlett O'Hara' has bright red blossoms and splashes of white on the leaves. 'Scarlet Star' displays many cerise flowers with central white stars. '

Ipomoea × multifida, cardinal climber.

![morning glory flowers]

Ipomoea tricolor 'Flying Saucer', morning glory.

Ipomoea tricolor • Morning Glory

❀ Sky-blue to purple

↕ 10'–12' ↔ 12"; plant 8"–12" apart.

This fast-growing twining vine, originally from Central and South America, is one of several species called morning glory. It has heart-shaped, slender-tipped light green leaves up to 4 inches long. It produces its recognizable 3-inch-wide funnel-shaped flowers either singly or in clusters of three to five blossoms in cymes.

Growing Tips See page 42.

Companion Plants Grow individual cultivars singly, or mix and match any of the color forms as desired. Plant carmine-flowered *Catharanthus* 'Pacifica Cherry', *Verbena* 'Obsession Coral Eye', or cherry-red dwarf snapdragon (*Antirrhinum* 'Montego Rose') at the base of *Ipomoea tricolor* 'Roman Candy'.

Cultivars Breeding has produced flower colors far beyond the familiar. *Ipomoea tricolor* 'Crimson Rambler' has red flowers with white throats. The 3-inch-wide flowers of 'Flying Saucer' are variably marbled in white and purple-blue with golden throats. 'Roman Candy' has cerise-and-white flowers and white-variegated leaves.

Annuals for Picking

Whether you are dashing off to a formal dinner party or a potluck lunch with friends, attending a birthday bash, or visiting a loved one in the hospital, what could be nicer than arriving with a fragrant bouquet of beautiful flowers from your garden? For optimum vase life, harvest flowers in the cool of the morning and immediately plunge the cut stems into a bucket of lukewarm water. For more details, see "Care of Fresh-Cut Annuals From the Garden," page 52.

Agastache Species • Giant Hyssops

🌸 Orange, pink, blue, white, apricot, rose, purple

↕ 12"–48" ↔ 12"–24"; plant 12"–24" apart.

The genus *Agastache* comprises many aromatic, perennial species indigenous to the dry, often hilly parts of China, Japan, the United States, and Mexico. Where they are not hardy, giant hyssops are cultivated as annuals, since they bloom profusely the first year from seed. They make excellent cut flowers, with minty-smelling foliage. Similar in appearance to their relatives in the genus *Salvia*, giant hyssops are erect, bushy plants with ovate to lance-shaped leaves 2 inches long. The flower spikes are 12 inches long and bear small, lipped, long-lasting tubular flowers in whorls. Many hyssops are attractive to hummingbirds, butterflies, and bees.

Growing Tips Cultivate giant hyssops in fertile soil. Sow seeds indoors four to six weeks before the last frost date. Pinch young plants to encourage bushiness. Alternately, take cuttings in fall, overwinter them indoors, and set them out the following spring. Keep flowers picked for constant bloom. In dry summers rust and mildew may be a problem.

Companion Plants Bring together giant hyssops with *Salvia splendens* 'Orange Zest', 18- to 24-inch sunflower (*Helianthus annuus* 'Dwarf Yellow Spray'), and *Zinnia* × *hybrida* 'Profusion Mixed'.

Cultivars and Related Species *Agastache* 'Pink Panther' shows light pink flowers on 24- to 30-inch plants. *Agastache* 'Apricot Sprite' is a terrific cultivar that produces 15- to 18-inch tasseled apricot florets. *Agastache cana,* hardy to Zones 5 to 10, produces strong, bushy, 24- to 30-inch plants that bear spikes of dark pink to rose-purple florets.

Ammi majus • Bishop's Weed

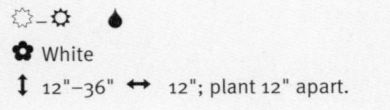

☼–☼ ⬥

❀ White

↕ 12"–36" ↔ 12"; plant 12" apart.

A native of southern Europe, North Africa, and Turkey, bishop's weed has become increasingly popular over the past few years. The umbels of white flowers are very similar to those of its cousin Queen Anne's lace, *Anthriscus sylvestris,* but are much larger and more delicate. The light green foliage is 6 to 8 inches long and much divided into finely toothed ovate leaflets.

Growing Tips Bishop's weed prefers fairly moist but well-drained, quite fertile soil. To avoid disturbing the slender taproot, sow the seeds, which germinate in about 15 days, right in the garden in early spring when the ground can be worked. Thin the seedlings to 1 foot apart. Stake them when they are about 3 to 4 inches tall. Pick as desired. Fully opened umbels may be removed from their stems and carefully dried horizontally; for best results use silica gel as a drying agent.

Companion Plants Combine bishop's weed with slate-pink *Cosmos* 'Versailles Tetra',

double-flowered pastel-colored poppy (*Papaver rhoeas* 'Angels Choir Mixed'), and blue lace flower (*Trachymene coerulea* 'Mixed Colours').

Cultivars and Related Species *Ammi majus* 'Green Mist' has a more refined growth habit than the species and has chartreuse flower buds opening into pure white; A. *visnaga* is green-flowered, with umbels 4½ to 5 inches across, on 3-foot-tall plants.

Antirrhinum majus
Common Snapdragon

☼–☼ ⬥

❀ Pink, purple, red, orange, yellow, white; bicolors

↕ 36" ↔ 12"; plant 10"–15" apart.

Snapdragons are easy to grow in cool-summer areas and are popular fall and winter annuals in warm regions. They decline rapidly in hot summer climates. Their dragon's-head-like flowers—long, upright racemes, or spikes, of five-lobed tubular blooms with a pouting lower lip—are among the best blooms for cutting. They are valuable vertical accents in mixed plantings and in containers.

Growing Tips Snapdragons do well in most soils. Sow seeds indoors eight to ten weeks before your last frost date. In mild-winter areas, sow outdoors in August or September in an out-of-the-way spot, then transplant when nights begin to turn cool. Snapdragons are susceptible to rust, so choose rust-resistant varieties and avoid overhead watering.

Companion Plants Combine dark-flowered varieties with *Mauranthemum paludosum* and English daisy (*Bellis perennis*). Pair the lighter shades with white sweet alyssum (*Lobularia maritima* 'Snow Crystals'); Iceland poppy (*Papaver nudicaule*

Ammi majus, bishop's weed.

Antirrhinum majus 'Rocket', common snapdragon.

'Wonderland') in pink, yellow, or white; and parsley (*Petroselinum crispum*).

Cultivars and Related Species There are dozens of cultivars with the original dragon's-head-like flowers, as well as open-flowered types with trumpet-shaped blooms and double-flowered forms; they range in height from tall to knee-high to dwarf.

Clarkia amoena • Satin Flower, Clarkia, Farewell to Spring

☼ – ☼ ⬤

❀ Lilac to reddish pink, usually with darker blotches in center

↕ 10"–30" ↔ 12"; plant 9" apart.

The genus *Clarkia*, native to western North America and South America, is grown for its jubilant ruffled, 2-inch-wide, single or fully double, somewhat mallow-like flowers held in racemelike clusters at the end of slender, leafy stems. The lance-shaped leaves are 2½ inches long.

Growing Conditions Satin flower prefers slightly acidic, moderately fertile, well-draining soil. Very rich soil encourages foliar growth at the expense of flower production. Sow seeds directly in the garden in early spring, thinning to 12 inches apart. Twiggy plant supports may be required in windy areas. Satin flower dislikes the heat and humidity of summertime and will do well in mountainous or woody areas. Keep the flowers picked for best results.

Companion Plants Combine satin flowers with flowering tobacco (*Nicotiana* 'Break-through Mixed'), pastel-flowered *Phlox drummondii* 'Phlox of Sheep', both of which are fragrant and tolerant of light shade.

Cultivars and Related Species The 30-inch-tall Grace Series has single lavender-pink, red, salmon-pink, or pink blossoms with contrasting centers. The Satin Series is an 8-inch-tall dwarf mix producing single flowers in various colors with contrasting centers or petal margins. 'Sybil Sherwood' has single salmon-pink flowers that fade to white at the edges.

Care of Fresh-Cut Annuals From the Garden

If fresh-cut flowers are to last, each type of flower must be harvested at the appropriate stage of development. Flowers with multiple buds on each stem should have at least one bud showing color and one bud starting to open before being cut. This is true for spike flowers (salvias, agastaches, snapdragons, stock, larkspur, and the like) as well as cluster flowers (annual baby's breath, lace flowers, satin flowers, verbenas, and silenes, for example). If gathered while they are still tightly budded, these flowers will not open in a vase of water. Flowers that grow on individual stems (such as calendulas, angel's trumpets, transvaal daisies, marigolds, sunflowers, and zinnias) should be cut when fully open.

Early morning is the ideal time to cut fresh flowers. The flowers have had the benefit of cool night air and morning dew. Their stems are filled with water and carbohydrates and are firm to the touch. Take a clean, sharp knife, clippers, or garden shears and cut flower and foliage about one inch from the bottom of the stem at an angle of about 45 degrees. When cut at an angle, the stem end provides

a large exposed area for the uptake of water, and the stem can stand on a point, which allows water to be in easy contact with the cut surface. To retard bacterial growth and extend the vase life of your flowers, completely remove any lower foliage that would be submerged in water.

Immediately plunge the flower stems in a plastic bucket filled with lukewarm water; about 100°F to 110°F is optimal. (The only exceptions are the stems of spring flower bulbs, such as hyacinths and tulips, which should be submerged in cold water.)

Freshly cut larkspur and delphinium arranged in a vase.

Flowers with rigid stems, such as cockscomb, satin flowers, marigolds, statice, and transvaal daisies, need only the diagonal cut to absorb maximum water. They should be left to take up lukewarm water with preservative for a minimum of one hour before arranging.

The stems of flowers with hollow stems, such as bells-of-Ireland, dahlias, and larkspur, need to be filled with water. Simply turn the flower upside down and fill the open cavity of the stalk with water. To keep the liquid in, you can plug the stem with a small piece of cotton and then place it in the vase. Or you can place your thumb over the opening at the bottom of the stem and then put it in the water. The water trapped inside will keep the stem strong and straight.

Flowers such as annual poinsettia and snow-on-the-mountain secrete milky latex sap that oozes into the water and clogs the vascular system of the other flowers in the container, preventing them from absorbing water. For this reason, the ends of the stems need to be seared. There are two ways to accomplish this: The first is to place the cut end of the precut flower stem in a cup of boiling water for about 30 seconds before placing it in the arrangement. Or you can apply a flame from a match or candle to the precut flower stem for about 30 seconds, and then place it in the arrangement.

Using preservatives definitely increases the longevity of cut flowers. Here's why: The main elements needed for flower survival are sugar, biocides, and acidifiers. In nature the sugar needed for nutrition is supplied by photosynthesis. Biocides are substances that combat bacteria and are necessary to maintain plant health. Acidifiers adjust the pH of the water, which increases the plant's water uptake. Preservatives are available commercially, but it's just as easy to make your own using the following recipe.

CUT-FLOWER PRESERVATIVE
Add the following ingredients to 1 quart lukewarm water:
1 teaspoon sugar
1 teaspoon household bleach
2 teaspoons lemon or lime juice

—*Rose G. Edinger*

Eustoma grandiflorum • Prairie Gentian

☼ ◔–◕

❀ Dark-centered pale purple

↕ 8"–24" ↔ 8"–12"; plant 8"–10" apart.

Recent breeding and selection regimens have produced scores of single and double cultivars of this Nebraska, Colorado, Kansas, and Texas native. Prairie gentian is a single-stemmed or branching annual with slightly fleshy, glaucous, oblong or ovate gray-green 5-inch leaves. During summer, broadly bell-shaped 2-inch, satin-textured flowers are borne on wiry stems either singly or in clusters from the leaf axils.

Growing Tips Start seeds indoors six weeks before the last frost date and set out plants when all danger of frost has passed in neutral to slightly alkaline soil. Initially, seedlings grow slowly. Water during dry spells. Twiggy plant supports are necessary. Keep the flowers picked for continuous bloom. Watch out for virus diseases, gray mold, and *Fusarium* wilt (discard infected plants; do not compost).

Companion Plants Try combining prairie gentian with pinks (*Dianthus chinensis* 'Frosty Mixed'), baby's breath (*Gypsophila elegans* 'Bright Rose'), and snapdragon (*Antirrhinum* 'Frosty Lavender Bells').

Cultivars and Related Species *Eustoma grandiflorum* 'Mermaid Extra Dwarf Mixed' bears pink-, white-, or black-centered blue flowers on dwarf 6-inch plants. 'Aloha Deep Red' grows 18 to 24 inches tall and holds rich red, silky blooms. 'Double Eagles Mixed' produces fully double creamy-white, rose, pink, and lavender flowers, which are extremely long lasting as cut flowers.

Gerbera jamesonii
Transvaal Daisy, Gerbera Daisy

☼ ◔

❀ Orange-scarlet rays and yellow disk

↕ 10"–24" ↔ 10"–24"; plant 12" apart.

This warm-temperate South African perennial daisy relative, usually cultivated as an annual in cooler climates, is easy to use and very long lasting in floral arrangements. It is vaguely dandelionlike in growth, but much larger in stature with a basal rosette of 6- to 18-inch, deeply lobed foliage that gives rise to 12- to 18-inch-tall leafless scapes terminating in a solitary flower. The daisylike flowers are single or double and 3½ to 5 inches across.

Growing Tips Sow seed of transvaal daisy six to eight weeks before the last frost in 3-inch pots and transplant after all danger of frost has passed into moderately fertile, slightly acid, very well drained soil. In areas with heavy clay soil, it's best to plant transvaal daisy in pots. Beware of overwatering. Keep picking flowers for bouquets or deadhead weekly to keep the plants in bloom. Before the first frost in fall, you can lift a few transvaal daisies, set them into 6- to 8-inch pots in well-drained soil, and place them in a southern or western window as winter-flowering houseplants.

Left: *Eustoma grandiflorum*, prairie gentian.
Opposite: *Gerbera jamesonii*, transvaal daisy.

White *Gypsophila elegans* 'Snow Fountain', baby's breath, mixed with pink and purple petunias.

Companion Plants Combine transvaal daisy with pink-flowered *Dahlia* 'Noreen', white-flowered snapdragon (*Antirrhinum* 'Royal Bride'), and red-flowered larkspur (*Consolida* 'Kingsize Scarlet').

Cultivars and Related Species *Gerbera jamesonii* 'California Giants' has single flowers in shades of yellow, apricot, orange, red, and pink. 'Dwarf Pandora Mixed' produces floriferous plants that bear three to six flower stems at any one time in shades of pink, yellow, red, white, and bicolors. 'Rainbow Mix' produces compact plants with flower heads 4 to 5 inches across in shades of red, rose, pink, orange, and white.

Gypsophila elegans • Baby's Breath

☼ ◌ ◌

✿ White, pink, rose, carmine

↕ 12"–24" ↔ 12"; plant 10" apart.

Every annual flower design or cutting garden needs a good-sized clump of annual baby's breath. Its airy, elegant texture lightens up any large-leafed, heavy-flowered planting and acts as a diaphanous halo to show off other blossoms. A native of southern Ukraine and Turkey, baby's breath is an erect branching annual with narrow, linear lance-shaped gray-green foliage ¾ to 1½ inches long. It produces a profusion of 4-petaled, star-shaped ½-inch flowers borne on 4-inch branched panicles that are held on upright stalks.

Growing Tips Cultivate baby's breath in deep, light, well-drained, slightly alkaline soil. Sow seeds directly into the garden in early spring and thin them to 10 inches apart. Plants blossom six weeks from seed but only for a short time, so start successive crops every three weeks throughout the growing season. In a windy site, baby's breath will often need twiggy plant supports.

Companion Plants Use baby's breath as a background for cultivars of your favorite annuals that need similar cultural conditions. Try it with satin flower (*Clarkia* *amoena* subsp. *lindleyi*), pinks (*Dianthus chinensis*), *Erysimum perofskianum,* and prairie gentian (*Eustoma grandiflora*).

Cultivars and Related Species The classic *Gypsophila elegans* 'Bristol Fairy' displays large, double white flowers up to half an inch across. 'Carminea' has handsome deep carmine-pink blossoms, as does as the exceptional selection 'Red Cloud'.

Lagurus ovatus • Hare's-Tail Grass

🌸 Pale green, often purple-tinged when immature, ripening to pale, creamy buff

↕ 20" ↔ 12"; plant 4" apart.

A native of the Mediterranean region, hare's-tail grass is a charming annual named for its fluffy 2½-inch panicles that look just like a bunny's tail. It is an indispensable fresh or dried cut flower. The linear, light green leaves vary from 8 to 12 inches long. Throughout the summer it bears densely furry, ovoid to oblong spike-like panicles. For best effect, mass the plants in clumps or borders.

Growing Tips Sow seeds directly into the garden in early spring in light, sandy soil, thinning the seedlings to 4 inches apart. Cut the flower heads at any time for fresh arrangements. Alternatively, harvest the fluffy panicles just before they're fully ripe on dry mornings and hang them to dry. They absorb dyes well.

Companion Plants Pair hare's-tail grass with other annual cousins, including little quaking grass (*Briza minor*) and rattlesnake chess (*Bromus briziformis*), or with *Gazania* 'Kiss White' Series.

Cultivars and Related Species *Lagurus ovatus* 'Nanus' is far more compact, at 5 inches tall.

Lathyrus odoratus • Sweet Pea

🌸 Just about any color except yellow

↕ 6' ↔ 12" for climbing types; ↕ 18" ↔ 24" for bushy types; plant 12"–15" apart.

Sweetly scented, old-fashioned cultivars of this relative of the garden pea are beginning to come back into style; for a while, hybridizers had put perfume on the back burner and focused on larger, more colorful flowers. Modern dwarf or "bush" cultivars are available, but climbing types are still the most common. Sweet peas make vast quantities of magnificent cut flowers with a sweet, honeylike perfume.

Growing Tips How to grow sweet peas depends on your climate. In mild-winter regions with hot summers, sow seeds outdoors in fall and enjoy the blooms in winter and spring. In areas with cool summers

Lathyrus odoratus, **sweet pea.**

(with nights usually below 75°F), sow in late fall or very early spring, as soon as the soil can be worked. Sweet peas are most challenging in locations with cold winters and hot summers. In these areas, sow seeds indoors in a cool but sunny spot and transplant seedlings outdoors in early to mid-spring. Sweet peas prefer humus-rich soil, so work in plenty of compost before planting. Regular harvesting of cut flowers and foliar applications of fertilizer are helpful in maintaining bloom.

Companion Plants Sweet alyssum (*Lobularia maritima*) 'Easter Bonnet' Series or *Nemesia strumosa* 'KLM' makes a lovely low border in front of bushy sweet peas.

Cultivars and Related Species The lightly scented *Lathyrus odoratus* 'Early Multiflora' in white, scarlet, and a variety of pinks and blues makes great cutting flowers. The Knee-Hi group is an attractive bushy type. In warmer climates, plant the heat-resistant Cuthbertson type.

Linaria maroccana
Toadflax, Baby Snapdragon

✿ Violet-purple, occasionally pink or white; lower lip of flower marked yellow to orange, and lighter at the center

↕ 9"–24" ↔ 6"; plant 4"–6" apart.

Hailing from Morocco, this species of toadflax is very similar in appearance to its cousins the snapdragons (*Antirrhinum*). This is an erect, sticky-haired annual with alternate, narrowly linear light green foliage to 1½ inches long. During summer it bears informally relaxed racemes of 2-lipped flowers up to ½ inch long. Toadflax is terrific for the rock garden or alpine trough.

Growing Tips Sow seeds directly in the garden in light, well-drained, preferably sandy soil as soon as the ground can be

worked, and thin the seedlings to 4 to 6 inches apart. Remember that the terminal tip of the raceme will bend upward when arranged horizontally. Keep flowers picked for ultimate bloom.

Companion Plants Toadflax looks great paired with Chinese-houses (*Collinsia bicolor* 'Surprise'), California poppy (*Eschscholzia californica* 'Buttermilk' or Rose Chiffon'), or *Petunia* 'Prism Candy Mixed'.

Cultivars and Related Species The dwarf mix *Linaria maroccana* 'Fairy Bouquet' attains 9 inches in height and holds ¾-inch flowers in yellow, rose-pink, salmon-pink, orange carmine, lavender, and white. 'Northern Lights' has the same color palette as 'Fairy Bouquet', but at 24 inches tall, it is larger, and it flowers longer. 'White Pearl' is 9 inches tall and has pure-white blossoms up to ¾ inch long.

Malope trifida • Annual Mallow

✿ Pink, violet-blue, or white, all heavily veined with purple

↕ 36" (but newer cultivars may be far shorter) ↔ 9"; plant 9" apart.

This beautiful 2- to 3-foot-tall mallow, originally from North Africa and Spain, is cultivated for its lovely long-stalked, broadly trumpet-shaped flowers, which are 2 to 3 inches wide. The mid-green hairy leaves are usually lobed and 4 inches across.

Growing Tips Sow seeds directly into the garden as soon as the ground can be worked. Annual mallow self-sows freely, but seedlings of named selections may not come true from seed. Cut frequently to promote a longer period of flowering. Provide twiggy supports in a windy site. Annual mallow prefers full sun but tolerates light shade in fertile, moisture-retentive, well-drained soil.

Malope trifida 'Purple Spanish Mallow', annual mallow.

Companion Plants Cultivate annual mallow in the front or middle of the mixed annual border behind deep cherry-red *Lobelia* 'Rosamund' or 'String of Pearls', a mixed offering with white, carmine, rose, and blue flowers on mounded plants. Also try it with geranium (*Pelargonium* 'Vogue Appleblossom').

Cultivars and Related Species 18- to 24-inch-tall *Malope trifida* 'Glacier Fruits' is a voluptuous combination of pure white, cerise, carmine, and red. 'Vulcan' produces abundant 3-inch magenta-pink blossoms. 'White Queen' bears 2-inch pure-white flowers.

Nicotiana langsdorffii
Flowering Tobacco

☼–☼ ◖

✿ Apple-green flowers with blue anthers

↕ 5' ↔ 14"; plant 12" apart.

Originally from Brazil, this species of flowering tobacco is an annual bearing a basal rosette of ovate leaves to 10 inches long. It bears nodding, slender panicles of tubular 2-inch-long flowers, which are quite attractive to bees, butterflies, and hummingbirds.

Growing Tips Generally speaking, all *Nicotiana* species prefer fertile, moist but well-drained soil. Sow the seeds directly into the garden in mid-spring or start them indoors six weeks before the last frost date, thinning them to 1 foot apart. Flowering tobacco needs a well-placed hidden plant support system. Aphids, leafminers, caterpillars, and spider mites as well as mosaic viruses can be problematic.

Companion Plants Combine flowering tobacco with fragrant mignonette (*Reseda* 'Fragrant Beauty'), *Petunia* 'Prism Sunshine', and *Hypoestes* 'Confetti White'.

Nicotiana langsdorffii, flowering tobacco.

Cultivars and Related Species Currently, few cultivars of *Nicotiana langsdorffii* are available. 'Cream Splash' is one of them. For *Nicotiana alata,* see page 39. For *Nicotiana sylvestris,* see page 40.

Papaver nudicaule • Iceland Poppy

☼ ◌–◆

✿ Yellow, orange, salmon, rose, pink, cream, white

↕ 10"–24" ↔ 8"–12" (basal leaves); plant 10"–12" apart.

Native from subarctic regions south to mountainous parts of Colorado and Eurasia, Iceland poppy is a perennial grown as a half-hardy annual. It prefers cool weather, and its vivid saucer-shaped flowers are popular for winter and early-spring color in California, the Southwest, and the deep South.

Growing Tips Poppies do not transplant well, so sow them directly in a well-draining flower bed or start them indoors in peat pots. They need light to germinate, so don't cover the seeds; just press them lightly into the soil with the back of your hand. Where winters are mild, sow outdoors in late summer or early autumn, or set out plants in autumn. In cool climates, sow seed in early spring for summer flowers. Cut flowers often to prolong bloom. Plants exude a milky substance; sear cut stem ends before placing them in water.

Companion Plants For a refreshing display of cool-season color, try Iceland poppy with common snapdragon (*Antirrhinum majus*), *Mauranthemum paludosum*, white sweet alyssum (*Lobularia maritima* 'Carpet of Snow'), pansy (*Viola* × *wittrockiana*), and parsley (*Petroselinum crispum*).

Cultivars and Related Species *Papaver nudicaule* 'Champagne Bubbles' is widely available in mixed shades of orange, yellow, white, pink, apricot, and cream blooms. 'Wonderland', though shorter, is usually available in single shades. *Eschscholzia californica*, California poppy, is good to seed in fall in warm climates, where winter temperatures don't drop below freezing.

Annuals for Shade

Gardeners view shade in two divergent lights—no pun intended. It may be a spot sought after to escape the searing summer rays—a dappled nook or sheltered corner perfect to cool off and relax in. But it may also be the bane of a metropolitan gardener faced with a cavernous courtyard shrouded by towering skyscrapers, where cultivating even the most modest planter box becomes a serious challenge. Likewise, too much shade may frustrate the suburban gardener whose yard is cast into perennial gloom by a neighbor's ancient shade trees. Whether you regard shade as something to relish or to overcome, this chapter will introduce some alternatives to the ubiquitous busy lizzies and wax begonias.

Bacopa cordata • Water Hyssop

☼–☼ ⬤

✿ Snowy white, light blue-violet, lavender-blue

↕ 3" ↔ 12"–18"; plant 10" apart.

A creeping, half-hardy species indigenous to coastal areas of southeast North America southward to Central America, water hyssop took the gardening world by storm when it was introduced into cultivation two decades or so ago. At last there was a rambling, flowering alternative to *Vinca minor* for borders and hanging baskets in moist shade! The plant has ½-inch or so ovate, somewhat fuzzy leaves supported by slender wiry stems. It produces ¼- to ½-inch-wide flowers throughout the growing season.

Growing Tips Put out rooted cuttings or young plants when the soil is thoroughly warmed in fertile but well-drained soil. High-nitrogen fertilizer supplemented with chelated iron helps keep the foliage green. Hardy to Zones 9 to 11.

Companion Plants Use *Bacopa* 'Blue Showers' with yellow-flowering *Impatiens* 'African Queen' or 'Seashells Yellow' and blue-flowered *Torenia fournieri* for an electric display that will liven up any moist, shady spot.

Cultivars and Related Species *Bacopa cordata* 'Snowstorm' has larger white flowers than the species and is disease-resistant and heat-tolerant. 'Blue Showers' has light blue-violet flowers, and 'Gold & Pearl' has green-and-gold-variegated foliage.

Begonia Hybrids
Cane-Stemmed Group

❋–☼ ◐

✿ Light pink, rose-pink, dark coral-pink, salmon-pink to orange

↕ 24"–36" ↔ 24"; plant 18" apart.

Most familiar as houseplants, these upright-growing fibrous-rooted begonias were derived from several, mostly Brazilian, species. They have slender bamboolike stems with regularly spaced swollen nodes and handsome broad, asymmetrical, often deeply toothed or lobed leaves that are often speckled with silver. Showy clusters of single or double flowers (which sometimes are slightly fragrant) are produced in terminal cymes as wide as 8 inches across in spring and summer. They make spectacular vertical additions to pots and borders and bring a refreshing style to the shade garden. Or try them in ornate flower pots to flank a shaded entranceway.

Growing Tips Cane-stemmed begonias prefer compost-rich, well-drained neutral to slightly acidic soil. If grown in deep shade,

some of the leaf markings may be lost and the canes become weak. When the soil is thoroughly warmed in spring, set out young plants or rooted cuttings that have been hardened off. During the season, cut overly long canes back to two or three buds, as the plants tend to get leggy and drop their bottom leaves. Take softwood cuttings in summer and move them inside as houseplants. Indoors, watch out for spider mites, scale, and mealybugs.

Companion Plants Mix with ferns, caladiums, and *Achimenes* for a colorful display.

Cultivars and Related Species *Begonia* 'Esther Albertine' is a large selection, growing to 8 feet tall and 6 feet wide and bearing deeply cut, silver-splashed apple-green 8- to 11-inch leaves and huge cymes of light pink flowers. 'Irene Nuss' has 8-inch-long wavy-margined leaves that are bronze above and red beneath, with cymes of 1½-inch, dark coral-pink blossoms. 'Orpha C. Fox' bears 6-inch-long gray-green leaves speckled with silver and maroon beneath and cymes of rose-pink 1¼-inch flowers.

Fuchsia Species and Cultivars
Fuchsias

❋–☼ ◐

✿ Pure white to pastel pink, hot pink, carmine, cerise, rose-pink salmon-pink; red, magenta, dark purple

↕ 6"–12' ↔ 8"–4'; plant 8"–12" apart.

There are about 100 species and more than 6,000 hybrids and cultivars of this genus of shrubs and trees native to Central and South America and New Zealand. Often treated as annuals in cooler climates, they are cherished for their distinctive, often bi-colored single, semidouble, or fully double tubular flowers, which

Begonia 'Orpha C. Fox'.

Fuchsia **in a hanging basket.**

appear more or less continually from summer to autumn. Fuchsias may grow upright and be used as border and container plants or be trained as standards and fans. Or they may trail and be used for hanging baskets, troughs, window boxes, and footed urns or be trained as weeping standards.

Growing Tips Grow fuchsias in fertile, well-drained soil. Fertilize weekly during active growth and flowering. They will not tolerate summer's high heat and humidity or drought and prefer cooler, less humid areas. Root softwood cuttings in spring and semiripe cuttings in late summer with bottom heat. Deadhead fertile cultivars to encourage continuous bloom and prevent fruit formation. If faded blooms are left alone, succulent edible ¾-inch-long red to purple berries develop. Overwinter plants in a greenhouse or on a cool windowsill with filtered light. Fuchsias require a winter dormancy period during which they are kept barely moist.

Companion Plants Team fuchsias with tuberous begonias, *Begonia* Tuberhybridacultorum group, such as white-flowered 'Billie Langdon', or *Begonia* 'Non-Stop', which is a little easier to grow. Or combine them with ferns, such as brake fern (*Pteris*), *Nephrolepis*, or *Cyrtomium,* for foliar effect.

Cultivars and Related Species *Fuchsia* 'Annabel' is a free-flowering upright type and produces medium-size fully double white blossoms with pink-striped white tubes, pink-flushed white sepals, and pink-veined white corollas on 12- to 24-inch-wide plants. Cultivars with variegated leaves include 'Celebration', 'Golden Marinka', and 'Jack Stanway'. 'Phyllis' is a vigorous upright selection that displays masses of small to medium semidouble flowers with waxy, cerise-flushed rose-red tubes and sepals and rose-cerise corollas on 3- to 5-foot plants. 'Red Jacket' is a free-flowering trailer, bearing large, fully double flowers that have bright red tubes and sepals and white corollas.

Impatiens 'African Queen'.

Impatiens 'African Queen'
Impatiens

☼ ◆
❀ Golden yellow with red veins in the center
↕ 21" ↔ 10"–12"; plant 10" apart.

A sensational, relatively recent introduction, *Impatiens* 'African Queen' offers a fantastic breakthrough in flower shape and color. Generally speaking, this cultivar has flattened, shell-shaped 1-inch flowers that sport a short spur. The lanceolate foliage is a bright golden-green. Use this plant in great sweeps to brighten up shaded beds, or mass it in containers on either side of an entranceway.

Growing Tips Cultivate *Impatiens* 'African Queen' in compost- or manure-enriched, moisture-retentive but well-drained soil. Surface-sow seeds six to eight weeks before the last assured frost date. Take softwood cuttings in spring and early summer. In fall, move plants into a cool greenhouse for overwintering. They are susceptible to spider mites, whiteflies, and mealybugs indoors.

Companion Plants Team *Impatiens* 'African Queen' with golden-leafed coleus (*Solenostemon* 'Greening's Yellow' or 'Greening's Gold') and upright-growing orange-red-flowered *Fuchsia* 'Koralle' or apricot-flowered *F.* 'Aurora Superba'.

Cultivars and Related Species The 20-inch-tall *Impatiens* 'African Orchids' Series looks more like *Impatiens auricoma* except that the flowers are slightly broader. Flowers range from pastel apricot, red-yellow, and red-orange flushed with hints of lavender and purple. The 'Seashell Beach Party Collection' is intermediate between 'African Queen' and *Impatiens walleriana*, with a less wild, more domesticated look and shell-shaped flowers ranging from pale yellow to peach, apricot, and papaya-pink.

Impatiens niamniamensis 'Congo Cockatoo' • Impatiens

☼ ◐

✿ Bright orange and yellow

↕ 36" ↔ 14"; plant 12" apart.

This particular impatiens is relatively rare in cultivation, but it is well worth the trouble to seek it out. It is a native of tropical Africa from Cameroon south to Angola and east to southwest Kenya and northwest Tanzania. It is an erect-growing species and rather gaunt in shape with 2- to 9-inch-long alternate, long-petioled, elliptic or lanceolate dark green glossy foliage and rather large pendulous flowers.

Growing Tips See *Impatiens* 'African Queen'.

Companion Plants Combine *Impatiens niamniamensis* 'Congo Cockatoo' with small-leafed *Caladium* 'White Wing' or 'Gingerland' and red-haired *Begonia* 'Fireflush' or orange-flowered *B.* 'Orange Rubra'.

Cultivars and Related Species *Impatiens tinctoria,* a native of Ethiopia, southern Sudan, and southern Zaire, is a tuberous-rooted species. It is an amazingly vigorous grower that can attain 7 feet in height and a width of 3 feet. Its scented, white-lipped 2½-inch flowers are borne in racemes throughout the summer. Overwinter the tubers like dahlia tubers to replant the following spring.

Ionopsidium acaule
Violet Cress, Diamond Flower

☼ ◐

✿ White, lilac, and violet

↕ 24"–42" ↔ 36"–54"; plant 36" apart.

This charming but short-lived little annual is relatively obscure in cultivation. A native of Portugal, violet cress is grown for its fragrant four-petaled cruciferous flowers that appear throughout the summer on tiny, tufted plants. The leaves are rounded-ovate and held in rosettes. It is a plant for the shaded rock garden or trough plantings. It is also grown between paving stones or in crevices or used as an edging plant in shaded sites, where it will usually self-sow.

Growing Tips Sow seed directly into the garden in spring and summer, and in fall as well in areas that experience only light frosts (23°F), in rich, well-drained soil in a cool site. Plants will bloom about six weeks after germination. Violet cress resents summer's high heat and humidity and will only succeed in northern areas where summers are cool. It is hardy to Zone 9.

Companion Plants Pair violet cress with monkey flower (*Mimulus* × *hybridus* 'Andean Nymph'), which grows to 8 inches tall and bears open-throated ivory to white blossoms blotched or speckled with vari-

Impatiens niamniamensis **'Congo Cockatoo'.**

ous shades of pink, or try it with 18-inch-tall pouch flower (*Calceolaria mexicana*), which has yellow, pouchlike blossoms.

Cultivars and Related Species None.

Montia perfoliata
Claytonia, Miner's Lettuce

☼ ◗
◉ Tiny white flowers above loosely funnel-shaped leaves
↕ 10" ↔ 10"; plant 6" apart.

Claytonia is a North American native often found growing wild around abandoned farmsteads, prospector's cabins, and mining camps throughout the American West. The leaves have 10-inch-long petioles and are unusually formed, being both loosely triangular and nearly funnel-shaped with tiny five-petaled flowers produced in little racemes emerging from the center of the leaf. As a cut-and-come-again annual vegetable, the succulent young leaves, stems, and flowers are excellent eaten in tossed salad, and the older leaves can be cooked as a potherb.

Growing Tips Sow seeds directly in the garden in early spring in fertile soil in a lightly shaded area. Thin the seedlings to 6 inches apart. Claytonia prefers cool summers and will become lax in areas with high heat and humidity. Or cultivate it in pots on a cold bright windowsill or in a cold frame as a wintertime source of greens.

Companion Plants Combine claytonia with dwarf, 6- to 12-inch-tall, white-leafed *Caladium* 'Jackie Suthers', double white *Impatiens walleriana* 'Carousel White', and any of the silver-variegated brake ferns (*Pteris*).

Cultivars and Related Species 'Emerald Green' has a very open growth habit and bright dark green sturdy leaves that resist bruising. 'Lanceleaf' has long narrow leaves with a golden-reddish tinge and flowers that have purplish markings. 'Miner's Pick' is a large fast-growing cultivar with a distinctive upright growth habit.

Torenia fournieri
Torenia, Wishbone Flower

☼ ◗
✿ Lilac-blue with deep purple lower lips and yellow throats
↕ 4"–12" ↔ 4"–10"; plant 6"–8" apart.

Originally from Southeast Asia, torenia was another plant that rocked the gardening world two decades ago with the new textures and colors it offered for the shade garden. It is an erect, long-stalked annual that bears pointed 1½- to 2-inch-long ovate to narrowly ovate light green leaves. It is adored for its abundant 1½-inch-long pansylike flowers, which are tubular and become open-throated as they mature.

Montia perfoliata, claytonia.

Torenia fournieri, torenia.

Use the shorter cultivars of torenia as a border or edging plant or in pots. Try the trailing varieties in hanging baskets and footed urns, or use them to soften the hard edges of containers.

Growing Tips Cultivate torenia in fertile, well-drained soil. Start seeds indoors ten weeks before the last assured frost date. Germination takes 15 to 20 days. Pinch out growing tips to encourage branching. Transplant into the garden a few weeks after the last frost, when the soil has warmed up.

Companion Plants Team up *Torenia* 'Summer Wave Blue' with water hyssop (*Bacopa* 'Blue Showers') and violet and brown-leafed coleus (*Solenostemon* 'Violet Ruffle'), or play up the yellow flower of *Torenia* 'Tiger Moon' with *Bacopa* 'Gold & Pearl' and yellow-leafed coleus (*Solenostemon* 'Golda').

Cultivars and Related Species *Torenia fournieri* 'Happy Faces Mix' combines pastel shades of pale pink, rose, and light blue flowers marked with darker hues on the petals. 'Summer Wave Blue' is a relatively new heat- and sun-resistant introduction with blue bicolor, snapdragonlike flowers on trailing plants. 'Summer Wave Amethyst' is also trailing but has bicolor dark and light burgundy blossoms. 'Pink Moon' bears pink and white bicolor flowers, and 'Tiger Moon' has golden-yellow and deep plum flowers on compact plants.

Tender Tropicals

For those gardeners who think the trend toward using tropical plants as annuals is new, think again. Victorian gardeners started the practice and came up with some wild color combinations in the process. Today we still appreciate these same tender beauties, along with new cultivars that have also made their way into our gardens.

Abutilon × *hybridum* • Flowering Maple

✱ – ☼   ◖

✿ Yellow, white, orange, pink, red

↕ 24" ↔ 10" for upright hybrids; ↕ 8"
↔ 10" for trailing hybrids; plant 8"–10" apart.

Plants in the genus *Abutilon* get their common name from the maple-leaf shape of the foliage. There are upright species perfect for the border or container and trailing forms, which look best in hanging baskets. Leaves can be solid green or variegated with yellow splotches or white edging. And if that isn't enough to choose from, the delicate, crepe-paper-textured flowers can be hanging and bell-shaped or upright and cup-shaped.

Growing Tips Flowering maple grows best in rich soil and should be fertilized weekly. Propagation is easily done from cuttings (see page 101). Consider overwintering flowering maple indoors; it makes an excellent houseplant for a sunny, cool window. (But keep an eye out for whiteflies.)

Opposite: *Abutilon* × *hybridum*, flowering maple.

Companion Plants Underplant flowering maple with something that brings out its flower color: Use *Plectranthus argentatus* with a white flowering maple or parrot leaf (*Alternanthera ficoidea*) with orange- or red-flowered varieties.

Cultivars and Related Species *Abutilon megapotamicum* is a weeping species with yellow flowers that have red centers and inflated red calyces. The leaves are green and yellow. *Abutilon pictum* 'Thompsonii' is an upright flowering maple; it has salmon-colored flowers and green and yellow foliage.

Amaranthus caudatus
Love-Lies-Bleeding

☼   ◖

✿ Red, yellow, purple, and bronze

↕ 3'–5' ↔ 24"–36"; plant 24" apart.

A dramatic plant deserves a dramatic name, and love-lies-bleeding lives up to its moniker. The 6- to 12-inch-long thick,

Amaranthus caudatus, love-lies-bleeding.

dangling flower tassles look like chenille. They last for weeks on the plant and also make unusual dried specimens.

Growing Tips Heat-tolerant love-lies-bleeding is not picky about soil quality. However, in rich soil colors may be less vibrant. Start seeds indoors in individual peat pots six to eight weeks before the last frost and transplant the seedlings after the last frost. Plants already in flower do not transplant well.

Companion Plants Nothing can compete with love-lies-bleeding, so plant it alongside a plant that can complement it, like snake plant (*Sansevieria trifasciata* 'Laurentii').

Cultivars and Related Species *Amaranthus caudatus* 'Intense Purple' has narrow purple leaves and red-purple tassles. *Amaranthus tricolor*, joseph's coat, is grown for its foliage, which is bronze, red, and green.

Celosia argentea • Cockscomb

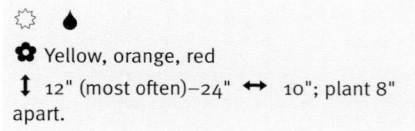

☼ ◗

❀ Yellow, orange, red

↕ 12" (most often)–24" ↔ 10"; plant 8" apart.

This plant is wild! There are several interesting forms of cockscomb; all are topped with brightly colored, unusually shaped blooms. They make excellent cut flowers and have been used as bedding plants for more than a century. The plumed form, *Celosia argentea* Plumosa group has an open feathery infloresence that is 6 to 12 inches tall. The crested form, *C. argentea* Cristata group, has a rolled inflorescence, crinkled like brain tissue. It is 6 to 12 inches wide and looks like no other. You either love it or you hate it.

Growing Tips For best results, grow cockscomb in well-drained fertile soil enriched with compost. If your soil is nutrient poor, be sure to fertilize every other week. Sow seeds directly in the garden in early summer. Seedlings may not transplant well, so if you start seeds indoors, do it in peat pots that you can plant out individually. It's important never to transplant cockscombs already in flower. These will not fill out to create the vivid splash you're looking for.

Companion Plants For a remarkable show, interplant clumps of cockscomb with your favorite cultivar of the new, sun-tolerant coleus (*Solenostemon scutellarioides*). Alternatively, soften the bright colors of cockscomb by planting it next to one of the sedums with blue-gray foliage.

Cultivars and Related Species *Celosia argentea* Cristata group 'Amigo Mahogany Red' has dark purple foliage topped with maroon blooms. The flowers of 'Bombay Pink' have dark pink edges and light pink interiors. *Celosia argentea* Plumosa group 'New Look' is heavily branched and has bright red plumes on top of bronze foliage.

Codiaeum variegatum var. pictum
Croton

☼–☼ ◆

◕ Foliage in combinations of yellow, orange, red, and green

↕ 24"–36" ↔ 12"; plant 8"–10" apart.

Familiar as a houseplant in temperate zones, croton has for years been used as a landscape plant in tropical and subtropical climates. This plant is grown exclusively for its colorful foliage, which may change according to light intensity. Leaf shape is highly variable; glossy foliage can be oval, oak-leaf-shaped, twisted, or linear.

Growing Tips Croton needs rich soil. It does best with weekly fertilization. Colors are brightest in full sun, but it also grows in light shade. Handle the rootball carefully; croton may drop its leaves if the roots are manhandled. Propagate the plant from stem cuttings (see page 101). If you'd like to try overwintering this plant indoors, keep the following things in mind: 1. Choose the sunniest possible spot. This plant is used to intense outdoor light. 2. Place your plants on saucers of pebbles and add water to the level of the top of the pebbles. As the water evaporates, it raises the ambient humidity around the plant, yet the roots won't sit in water. 3. Check twice a week for signs of insects, which reproduce more quickly under hot, dry conditions. 4. New growth produced indoors may be less highly variegated than growth in full outdoor sun. Cut back less highly colored foliage before moving your plants outdoors in the spring.

Companion Plants Try surrounding a red-flowered *Hibiscus rosa-sinensis* standard with croton. Or use it under a gray-leafed specimen palm such as *Bismarkia nobilis* and bring the tropics to your garden.

Celosia argentea Cristata group, cockscomb.

Cultivars and Related Species *Codiaeum variegatum* var. *pictum* 'Carrierei' has striking red foliage marked with dark purple-green. 'Fascination' has exceptionally narrow leaves of yellow and red.

Cryptanthus bivattatus • Earth Star

☼ ◊

⊕ Foliage in shades of pink and white striped with green

↕ 2" ↔ 6"; plant 4"–6" apart.

Most bromeliads are epiphytes, better suited to growing on tree branches than in the ground. Earth star is a terrestrial species with about 4-inch-long leaves that radiate from the center of the plant. The star-shaped form makes for an unusual groundcover, hugging the soil and forming a carpet of color.

Growing Tips Earth star grows best in well-drained soil. Fertilize at half strength once a month, and be sure not to overwater. Too much water can cause the roots to rot. Earth star spreads by forming plantlets at the base of the mature plant. You can either let your earth stars spread, or remove a plantlet by gently pulling it apart from the mother plant once it has roots of its own. Lift these slow-growing plants before the frost and pot them up. Their small size makes them easy to overwinter on even a narrow windowsill.

Companion Plants Surround *Acorus gramineus* (a grasslike Japanese plant that grows to 12 inches high) with a clump of earth star. Or combine it with lilyturf (*Ophiopogon planiscapus* 'Arabicus').

Cultivars and Related Species *Cryptanthus fosteranus* is an exceptional beauty with copper-purple-green leaves and silvery zebra stripes. Foliage grows to about 6 inches in length.

Hoya carnosa, **wax plant.**

Hoya carnosa • Wax Plant

☼ – ☀ ◊

✿ Shades of pink

↕ 10' ↔ 24"; plant 8" apart.

A popular houseplant for years, wax plant is finally being appreciated as a garden plant. In the landscape it can be used as a groundcover or climbing vine, or in hanging baskets. Roots form along the stems, helping the plant crawl either horizontally or vertically. Mature plants flower freely, and the star-shaped two-toned flowers are quite fragrant, especially in the evening. Thick leaves are white and green, with patterns and shades of variegation depending on the cultivar. In high light, leaves can also be tinged with pink.

Growing Tips Wax plant grows best in well-drained soil. While it likes direct sun indoors, it should be protected from the hottest rays outdoors. It starts easily from cuttings (see page 101).

Companion Plants As a groundcover, plant wax plant at the base of banana yucca (*Yucca baccata*) or orpine (*Hylotelephium telephium* 'Arthur Branch'); or train it up a trellis or small shrub.

Cultivars and Related Species *Hoya australis* has larger, solid green leaves and its flowers are a delicate white. It is a vigorous climber. In a hanging basket, try *H. lacunosa*, whose fragrant perfume is strongest at night.

Mandevilla Species • Mandevilla Vines

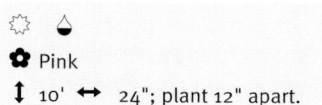

✿ Pink

↕ 10' ↔ 24"; plant 12" apart.

The several species and hybrid cultivars of *Mandevilla* differ most obviously in the appearance of their foliage. *Mandevilla* × *amabilis* has coarser, larger leaves with a prominent midrib and veins and is a strong climber; *M. splendens* (sometimes sold as *Dipladenia splendens*) has smaller, shinier leaves that lack the prominent venation of its cousin. It also has a more trailing growth habit. Flowers of both species are tubular with flared petals measuring about 2 inches across, and hummingbirds love them.

Growing Tips This vine blooms best in rich garden soil. If your soil is of average quality, feed it every other week. You may need to help mandevillas start climbing, but they will quickly take over on their own. Propagation is easiest from cuttings (see page 101). This vine is also an excellent houseplant if you can give it the warmth, sun, and humidity it requires.

Companion Plants Plant mandevilla with sweet-potato vine (*Ipomoea batatas* 'Blackie') for a bold climbing combo. On a tripod it makes an excellent container plant. Try surrounding it with *Scaevola aemula* or New Guinea impatiens (*Impatiens platypetala*) 'Magenta Solania'.

Cultivars and Related Species *Mandevilla* × *amabilis* 'Alice du Pont' is a readily available cultivar with 4-inch-wide, bright

Mandevilla × *amabilis* 'Alice du Pont', mandevilla vine.

pink blooms. *M. boliviensis* has 2-inch-wide white flowers with a yellow throat.

Musa 'Zebrina' • Ornamental Banana

☼–☼ ●

🌑 Huge leaves colored with burgundy splashes

↕ 5' ↔ 36"; plant 36" apart.

Ornamental banana makes an outstanding focal point in the border and also performs well in containers. This banana is not grown for its fruit, though there are a few fruiting varieties appropriate for the home garden.

Growing Tips Plant ornamental banana in well-drained soil and feed it weekly. Beware of windy locations, as the wide leaves may be shredded in high winds. A mature banana plant makes a dramatic specimen, so you may want to try overwintering it. You have several choices: Keep the plant in a sunny room and let it grow, or cut it back to within several inches of the soil level and store it in a cool dark place (where temperatures stay above freezing) until spring. Alternatively, dig up

Musa 'Zebrina', ornamental banana.

the roots and store them like the tubers of *Canna*. It's worth the effort to maintain a truly impressive specimen.

Companion Plants Surround ornamental banana with tufted fescue (*Festuca amethystina*) or lilyturf (*Ophiopogon planiscapus* 'Arabicus'). Or combine it with castor bean (*Ricinus communis*) to create a tropical jungle.

Cultivars and Related Species *Ensete ventricosum* 'Maurelii' is a banana plant with burgundy leaves splashed with dark green. Mature specimens can reach 12 to 15 feet. *Musa acuminata* 'Super Dwarf' is a green-leafed banana plant that grows to 3 feet tall and produces edible fruit at an early age, sometimes in its first year.

Opposite: *Passiflora coccinea*, passionflower.

Passiflora Species • Passionflower

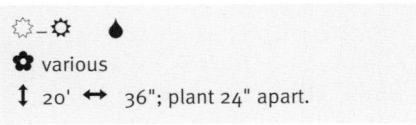

☼–☼ ●

❀ various

↕ 20' ↔ 36"; plant 24" apart.

Climbing via tendrils, passionflowers can easily cover a railing or trellis in one season. The flowers are layered and enormously elaborate and can grow to 5 inches across. These are quintessentially exotic blooms. There are numerous species to choose from, depending on your aesthetic and color scheme. All require approximately the same care, and all attract butterflies to your garden.

Growing Tips Passionflower grows best in rich garden soil and warm temperatures. Don't overfertilize or you'll encourage lush foliage growth at the expense of bloom. This plant is easily propagated from cuttings (see page 101). After a long summer outdoors, lift it, pot it up, and cut it back hard (to within a foot of the soil level). You can overwinter this plant in a southern or eastern window and plant it outdoors again next year. Some people grow it exclusively as a houseplant.

Companion Plants Intertwine passionflower vines with night-blooming moonflower (*Ipomoea alba*), to have a vine in bloom around the clock. Let it twine around small trees and shrubs, or plant it on a tripod in a container for vertical interest and surround it with a complementary trailing plant such as *Scaevola aemula* or *Verbena canadensis* 'Summer Blaze'.

Cultivars and Related Species Fragrant *Passiflora alata* has especially elaborate purple and pink flowers. *Passiflora caerulea* is a heavy bloomer and its blue and white flowers are fragrant. *Passiflora trifasciata* is grown for its foliage rather than its flowers, which are small, yellow, and not hugely remarkable. Leaves are purple and green and subtly beautiful.

Drought-Tolerant Bloomers

The plants in this chapter come from arid regions of the world. Once established in your garden, they make do with very little supplemental watering for the remainder of the season. They are especially useful in years of drought or in areas that are perennially dry, such as sandy slopes or seaside gardens whipped by desiccating winds. Also try them for a low-maintenance container garden.

Bougainvillea spectabilis; B. glabra
Bougainvillea

❀ Orange, white, magenta, or red bracts
↕ 30' ↔ 24"–36"; plant 24" apart.

If I were trapped on a desert island and could only have one plant, it would probably be *Bougainvillea*. It won't feed or clothe you, but oh, what a feast for the eyes. What most people think of as flowers are actually bracts, which surround the small white, true flowers inside them. *Bougainvillea* can have variegated or solid green foliage, and the stems are quite thorny, so be careful while handling. It's a sturdy vine that can grow on a trellis, in a hanging basket, or be trained as a standard.

Growing Tips This plant thrives in hot, dry climates; in fact, you'll reduce flowering if you give it too much water. Too much fertilizer or rich soil will encourage foliage growth but not flowers. Water a little more often only if you notice that the foliage

looks droopy. Plants flower on new growth, so pruning won't curtail bloom. In colder climates, cut back the vine at the end of summer and overwinter it in a southern window. In Zones 9 through 11, *Bougainvillea* can be grown as a perennial.

Companion Plants *Bougainvillea* comes in hot colors and mixes well with other vividly colored plants that can hold their own against this flamboyant vine. For a tropical feel, try planting it with bright-flowered *Hibiscus rosa-sinensis* or next to a *Bismarkia nobilis*, which has silver-blue fronds.

Cultivars and Related Species Solid-leaf *Bougainvillea* cultivars are usually more vigorous than those with variegated foliage: *Bougainvillea* 'California Gold', with yellow bracts, and 'Texas Dawn', with pink bracts, are extraordinary. 'Delta Dawn' combines variegated foliage with orange bracts. 'Raspberry Ice' is one of the most vigorous variegated cultivars, with outstanding magenta bracts. 'Thimba' also has variegated foliage, and bracts may be white and bright pink on the same plant.

Cleome hassleriana
Spider Flower, Cleome

☼–☼ ◌

❀ White, pink, lavender, magenta

↕ 4'–5' ↔ 24"; plant 12"–18" apart.

An excellent annual for the back of the border, tall spider flower moves gracefully in the wind, and the small spikes on the stems discourage animals from chewing on the plant. It has narrow leaves, which echo the linear form of the flower petals. Each flower head measures approximately 4 inches in diameter and is made up of numerous 4-petaled blooms.

Growing Tips Spider flower grows well in average soil and requires very little fertilizer. It branches without pinching and may need to be staked as it gets larger. It self-seeds prolifically in autumn and is also easy to start indoors from seed in early spring. Start seeds eight to ten weeks before the last frost in your area. This annual tolerates some cold and can be set outside two to three weeks before your last spring frost.

Companion Plants Spider flower mixes well with ornamental grasses such as feather reed grass (*Calamagrostis acutiflora stricta*), which shares its habit of swaying in the breeze. It looks especially impressive when planted in large masses of a single color. Try it with globe artichoke (*Cynara scolymus*) for dramatic contrast.

Cultivars and Related Species The *Cleome hassleriana* 'Queen' Series has been bred for strong color and a nice branching habit. It is readily available in nurseries as young plants or as seed.

Helichrysum petiolare
Licorice Plant, Curry Plant

☼–☼ ◌

◉ Woolly foliage in silver, chartreuse, soft gray-green; variegated silver and lime-green

↕ 24"–36" for groundcovers; 12"–18" for upright varieties ↔ 10"; plant 18" apart for groundcovers; 10" apart for upright varieties.

Licorice plant comes in numerous useful shapes and colors. Leaves and stems are woolly, and many cultivars do not flower; they are grown for their foliage alone. The neutral tones of the solid-colored licorice plant make it useful for linking contrasting parts of your garden. While you may not want the magenta blooms of rose moss (*Portulaca grandiflora*) bumping up against an orange-flowered shrub verbena (*Lantana camara*), a swath of chartreuse-leafed licorice plants links the two colors quite nicely. The best-known cultivars are groundcovers or trailing plants, but some have an upright growth habit.

Growing Tips Licorice plant grows well in sandy to average soils. Start it indoors six to eight weeks before the last frost, and plant it in the garden as soon as danger of

Cleome hassleriana 'Violet Queen', spider flower.

frost is past. Pinching the growing tips will encourage branching. The plant will get leggy if it doesn't get enough sun.

Companion Plants No exaggeration: Licorice plant goes with almost anything. Plant it along the edge of a container with *Scaevola aemula* and *Sanvitalia,* or use an upright cultivar to offset the dramatic burgundy foliage and salmon flowers of *Fuchsia* 'Gartenmeister'.

Cultivars and Related Species *Helichrysum petiolare* 'Icicles' has narrow, silvery upright foliage, while 'Limelight' has cascading leaves of chartreuse. 'Seabreeze' has variegated foliage of lime-green and silver.

Ixora coccinea; I. chinensis
Burning Love, Jungle Geranium

☼–☀ ◊

✿ yellow, orange, pink, red

↕ 12"–14" ↔ 12"–14"; plant 12" apart.

These tropical shrubs make excellent drought-tolerant annuals. Dark, glossy foliage sets off umbels of flowers 2 to 3

inches in diameter. The petal tips of *Ixora coccinea* are somewhat rounded, while those of *I. chinensis* are elongated and pointy. In cultivation, the two plants are easily confused. Both do well in containers, where their treelike shape makes them a natural focal point.

Growing Tips Burning love grows in almost any soil and benefits from occasional fertilization. To encourage bloom, plant it in full sun and keep it on the dry side. Propagate it from stem cuttings in spring. Since burning love is a slow grower, you may want to overwinter the plant in a sunny window, even though it will flower less indoors. If you keep your *Ixora* for several years, you'll be rewarded with a larger specimen plant.

Companion Plants Surround orange- or yellow-flowered burning love with sweet-potato vine (*Ipomoea batatas* 'Margarita') or licorice plant (*Helichrysum petiolare* 'Limelight') to show off its treelike form and glossy foliage. The pink- and red-flowered cultivars are best highlighted by the dark foliage of *Ipomoea batatas* 'Blackie' or one of the reddish trailing coleus (*Solenostemon scutellarioides*).

Cultivars and Related Species *Ixora casei,* giant *Ixora,* looks quite similar but grows to 10 feet tall. *I. hookeri* also reaches 10 feet in height and is very fragrant.

Pennisetum setaceum; P. villosum
Fountain Grass; Feather Grass

☼–☀ ◊

❂ Gracefully arching foliage and fluffy plumes

↕ 24"–36" ↔ 18"; plant 18"–24" apart.

Some *Pennisetum* species are perennials, but these two are annual ornamental grasses that work equally well as specimen plants

Ixora chinensis, burning love.

Pennisetum villosum 'Feathertop', feather grass.

or as backdrops for splashes of color in the border, forming dense, arching clumps. They are also valued for their graceful foliage, which moves nicely in a breeze. As medium-size grasses, these plants work well in the mid-border or in pots.

Growing Tips These two grasses grow best in fertile soil. Variegation will be highest in more intense light. They can be started from seed but are more frequently propagated by division.

Companion Plants Used as a backdrop, fountain grass supports the vibrant colors of daylilies (*Hemerocallis*) and garden montbretia (*Crocosmia*). In containers it looks wonderful underplanted with bright-colored star-cluster (*Pentas*), verbenas, and nasturtiums (*Tropaeolum*).

Cultivars and Related Species *Pennisetum setaceum* 'Rubrum' is a 36-inch-tall knockout with rich burgundy foliage and deep purple plumes. *Pennisetum setaceum* 'Red Bunny Tails' is similar in color and has a more compact growth habit, topping out at 24 inches. *Pennisetum villosum* 'Feathertop' grows to 15 inches tall, has slim green leaves, and large bright white flower plumes.

Phormium tenax • New Zealand Flax

☼–☼ ◊

● Foliage variegated with yellow, orange, or red tones

↕ 24"–36" ↔ 24"–30" (larger if overwintered); plant 24" apart.

The upright foliage of New Zealand flax comes in many shades and makes a superb vertical accent for containers and garden beds alike. This plant is used for the architectural value of its foliage. Leaves are swordlike and form a dense clump. Planted en masse, these plants make a bold statement. Singly, a specimen can be strategically placed to draw focus.

Growing Tips New Zealand flax grows best in rich soil and benefits from regular fertilization. Variegation is most intense in full sun. Overwinter it as a houseplant in a southern or western window.

Companion Plants New Zealand flax cultivars offset many plants with their shape, height, and foliage color. Try matching the variegation of the foliage with neighboring flowers, for example, thread-leaf coreopsis (*Coreopsis verticillata* 'Golden Shower') with *Phormium tenax* 'Yellow Wave' or star-cluster (*Pentas lanceolata* 'Butterfly Deep Pink') with *Phormium* 'Flamingo'. The bright-leafed parrot leaf (*Alternanthera ficoidea*) makes an excellent underplanting.

Cultivars and Related Species *Phormium* 'Apricot Queen' has green leaves with an apricot center and yellow borders. The leaves of *P.* 'Bronze Baby' are dark bronze. *Phormium* 'Flamingo' has green and bright pink foliage, and *P.* 'Yellow Wave' has green and yellow variegation.

Portulaca grandiflora 'Sundial Mix', rose moss.

Portulaca grandiflora
Rose Moss, Sun Moss, Moss Rose

☼ ◊

❀ Orange, yellow, white, magenta
↕ 3" ↔ 10"; plant 6" apart.

The fleshy, succulent leaves and stems of rose moss tell you right away that this plant can handle drought. It is a showy groundcover with double or single blooms. It's an excellent choice for containers, which tend to dry out quickly, and for the front of the border.

Growing Tips Sandy soil is best, but rose moss will grow in any garden soil that's not heavy clay. The seeds are so tiny that they tend to wash away if sown directly in the garden; instead, try starting them indoors and transplant when the soil has warmed. This is a very low-maintenance plant. Deadheading will tidy it up but is not necessary for continuous bloom.

Companion Plants The hot colors of rose moss combine well with equally intense *Verbena* cultivars. Try planting it with licorice plant (*Helichrysum petiolare* or *Helichrysum petiolare* 'Limelight') for outstanding foliage contrast. The blue foliage of tufted fescue (*Festuca amethystina*) also makes an excellent backdrop.

Cultivars and Related Species The closely related *Portulaca oleracea* is also very drought-tolerant. Flowers are yellow and smaller that those of *P. grandiflora*. The Yubi cultivars of *P. grandiflora* are available in a full range of vivid colors.

Scabiosa atropurpurea
Pincushion Flower

☼–☀ ◊

❀ Dark purple (almost black), dark red, pink
↕ 24"–36" ↔ 12"; plant 12" apart.

Most people know pincushion flower as a perennial, but some species are annual. *Scabiosa atropurpurea* makes a bold accent and excellent focal point. The 2-inch-wide flowers, borne on long stems, attract butterflies and are wonderful for cutting.

Growing Tips Plant pincushion flower in average garden soil. Start from seed indoors six to eight weeks before the last frost and transplant outside after danger of frost has passed. With conscientious deadheading it will bloom all season long.

Companion Plants The dark purple pincushion flower combines wonderfully with purple coneflower (*Echinacea purpurea*), pink or yellow coreopsis (*Coreopsis rosea* or *Coreopsis auriculata* 'Nana'), or *Gaura lindheimeri*.

Cultivars and Related Species *Scabiosa atropurpurea* 'Ace of Spades' is almost black-purple, sometimes described as deep maroon. 'Chile Sauce' is a dramatic dark red.

Opposite: A mix of dark purple and pink cultivars of *Scabiosa atropurpurea*, pincushion flower.

Verbena bonariensis, verbena bo.

Verbena bonariensis • Verbena Bo, Argentine Verbena, Brazilian Verbena

☼–☼ ◊

❀ Purple

↕ 24"–30" flower stalks ↔ 18"–24"; plant 8" apart.

Verbena bo has rosettes of foliage that hug the ground, topped by long-lasting flower heads borne on tall bloom stalks. Bees and butterflies love this flower, so try this one if you want to attract pollinators to your garden. Use it in the front or middle of the border. In front, you peer through the slim, graceful stems to whatever is planted behind it. In the middle, the purple flower heads seem to appear out of nowhere.

Growing Tips *Verbena bonariensis* grows in a wide range of soils. It is not a heavy feeder. Sow seeds directly in the garden in fall or early spring. Although this is an annual plant in cold climates, you may never have to replant, as it self-seeds freely. In Zones 8 through 11, verbena bo may be grown as a perennial. Note: *Verbena bonariensis* is being monitored as a potentially invasive plant in Washington State. For more information visit www.wa.gov/agr/weedboard.

Companion Plants Try *Verbena bonariensis* in front of white or pink coneflower (*Echinacea*) or next to obedient plant (*Physostegia virginiana*). Against a backdrop of ornamental grasses, the flowers stand out as they sway with the grasses.

Cultivars and Related Species The growth habit of *Verbena bonariensis* is very different from the related, more familiar trailing verbenas (*V. canadensis*). Cultural requirements, however, are similar. *Verbena canadensis* 'Summer Blaze' has bright red flowers, and *V. canadensis* 'Homestead' sports magenta-purple blooms.

Sensational Salvias

Up until a handful of years ago there were only a few salvia species cultivated by gardeners: *Salvia splendens,* scarlet sage, the riotous red backbone of so many industrial parks and cemetery landscapes; *S. farinacea,* mealy-cup sage; *S. leucantha,* Mexican sage; and the beautiful furry-leaved, silvery, short-lived perennial *S. argentea,* silver sage. But things have changed dramatically. New breeding regimens have produced some terrific new colors from some of the tired workhorses of the summer garden—elevating them to new aesthetic heights.

Salvia argentea • Silver Sage

☼ ⬡

◉ 8" to 12" toothed silver woolly leaves
↕ 12"–24" foliage rosette; 36"–48" flower stalks ↔ 15"–36"; plant 15"–30" apart.

Native to an area of southern Europe stretching from Portugal to Bulgaria, silver sage is a biennial or short-lived perennial that's hardy to Zones 5 to 8, but due to its dislike of soggy soils it does not always survive the winter. It is cherished for its handsome ovate to oblong, toothed silver woolly leaves, which are 8 to 12 inches long and 6 inches wide. Use this plant in borders, rock gardens, or containers.

Growing Tips Sharp drainage, friable soil, and excellent air circulation are crucial for success. Work a very small amount of lime into the soil around established plants. Remove the flower spikes to prolong the life of the plant, but ultimately leave a few to guarantee seed for future plants.

Companion Plants The gray woolly foliage looks particularly well against your favorite white or pastel pink, yellow, or purple flowers. Or for something different, team it up with other fuzzy-leafed plants such as dusty miller (*Senecio cineraria*), globe artichoke (*Cyanara scolymus*), velvet plant (*Gynura*), or *Plectranthus.*

Cultivars None.

Salvia argentea, silver sage.

Salvia chamaedryoides
Germander Sage

☼ ◐-◖

✿ Deep blue

↕ 12"–24" ↔ 24"; plant 20" apart.

This low, woody evergreen perennial species cultivated as an annual comes from the high, dry mountains of Texas and Mexico. It bears ¾-inch-long elliptic, finely scalloped medium green to gray-green leaves that are covered with fine hairs, giving the plant a sage-green appearance. During the heat of late summer and early fall it produces terminal racemes of 1-inch-long flowers. This is an excellent addition to the mixed dry border, wall garden, dry stream bed landscape or trough planting.

Growing Tips Loamy, quick-draining soil is mandatory for germander sage, which is drought-tolerant but flowers best with regular watering. Sow seeds indoors eight weeks before the last frost date and set out plants when the soil is thoroughly warmed. Remove spent inflorescences regularly to encourage flower production. Deer don't seem to find it appetizing. Hardy to Zones 8 to 10.

Companion Plants Team germander sage with heat- and drought-tolerant low-growing rosemary (*Rosmarinus* 'Santa Barbara'), which has deep blue flowers; *Gazania* 'Rose Kiss'; apricot-flowered giant hyssop (*Agastache* 'Apricot Sprite'); and tickseed (*Bidens* 'Golden Eye') for an eye-popping display.

Cultivars *Salvia chamaedryoides* 'Desert Green' has silver-green foliage.

Salvia coccinea
Scarlet Sage, Texas Sage

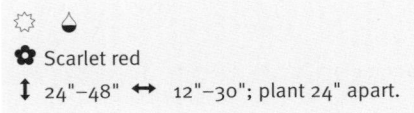

☼ ◐

✿ Scarlet red

↕ 24"–48" ↔ 12"–30"; plant 24" apart.

This erect, bushy tender perennial sage is distributed throughout tropical South America but appears to be most closely related to certain Mexican species. The 2½-inch dark green leaves are oval or heart-shaped, toothed, and hairy. From summer through autumn, slender, terminal spikes of ¾-inch flowers are produced. They are wildly attractive to hummingbirds, bees, and butterflies. This species adds a magical sparkle to the mixed bed or border and makes a particularly fine cut flower.

Growing Tips Scarlet sage needs decent garden soil enriched with compost and turkey grit or sand (to improve drainage). Sow seeds indoors six weeks before the last frost date and plant the seedlings out when the soil is thoroughly warmed. The plants will begin to bloom in late summer

Salvia coccinea 'Brenthurst', scarlet sage.

and will continue until stopped by frost. Keep spent inflorescences picked to encourage flower production. It is hardy to Zones 10 to 11.

Companion Plants Play up the scarlet red of this sage by combining it with wine-red transvaal daisy (*Gerbera* 'Jaimy'), orange-red dwarf Mexican sunflower (*Tithonia* 'Fiesta del Sol'), and yellow to orange to red fruited ornamental pepper (*Capsicum annuum*) 'Medusa'.

Cultivars *Salvia coccinea* 'Brenthurst' is a fine pink cultivar. 'Coral Nymph' produces coral-pink flowers on 16-inch-tall plants. 'Cherry Blossom' is shorter at 15 inches and has dark and light pink bicolored blooms. 'Lady in Red' bears bright red flowers on 16-inch-tall plants. 'Lactea' bears white flowers as does 'Snow Nymph'. 'Starry Eyed' displays white, red, or coral-pink blossoms.

Salvia discolor, **Andean sage.**

Salvia discolor • Andean Sage

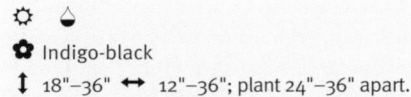

☼ ◊

✿ Indigo-black

↕ 18"–36" ↔ 12"–36"; plant 24"–36" apart.

A perennial denizen of a small region of Peru, Andean sage is usually cultivated as an annual. Sadly, it is still relatively rare in cultivation but the seeds or plants are well worth the trouble to track down. It has many white woolly stems arising from the base. The 2½-inch-long medium-green oblong-ovate, entire leaves are thickly white and woolly beneath and less hairy above. During warm spells in late summer and early autumn, Andean sage produces sticky terminal racemes of 1-inch flowers. Try this species as a specimen plant in containers.

Growing Tips Deep friable garden soil lightened with compost is needed for Andean sage. Start seed indoors six weeks

before the last frost date and set out plants when the soil is thoroughly warmed. This species usually requires a twiggy support system. Hardy to Zones 9 to 10.

Companion Plants If you would like to combine Andean sage with other plants, play up its indigo-black flowers and pistachio-green calyces by using black-leafed coleus (*Solenostemon* 'Black Cloud'), annual pinks (*Dianthus* 'Black & White') and purple-black-flowered sweet william (*Dianthus barbatus* 'Sooty').

Cultivars None.

Salvia farinacea • Mealy-Cup Sage

☼ ◊

✿ Deep lavender-blue

↕ 12"–30"; 36"–48" in warmer areas ↔ 12"; 24" in warmer areas; plant 24"–36" apart.

This old favorite perennial grown as an annual is native from central and eastern Texas to New Mexico and parts of neighboring Mexico. A dependable, trouble-free plant with a neat, tidy habit, it can be counted upon to bloom continuously. It has white mealy stems and 3-inch-long pointed, lanceolate foliage that is downy beneath. The species name, *farinacea*, is derived from the Latin for "flour" and alludes to the mealy-looking dusting that covers the inflorescences. From summer through autumn mealy-cup sage bears long terminal or axillary spikes of ¾-inch flowers, which are wonderful either picked for fresh arrangements or dried for craft projects.

Growing Tips Insect- and disease-resistant mealy-cup sage needs fast-draining soil enriched with compost. Start seed indoors six weeks before the last frost and set seedlings outdoors 1 foot apart when frost has passed. Seeds germinate in about 15 days. Pruning or pinching is not necessary. Hardy to Zones 8 to 10, mealy-cup sage will often perennialize farther north if it is grown in very well drained soil and winters are mild.

Companion Plants Set the blue shades of this sage off with 3-foot-tall semidwarf *Cosmos* 'Daydream', which displays lovely

light pink and dark pink bicolored flowers, along with 30-inch-tall *Zinnia* 'Oklahoma Golden Yellow' and snapdragon (*Antirrhinum* 'Labella Pink'), which is a rich rose-pink.

Cultivars *Salvia farinacea* 'Rhea' is compact at 14 inches and has intense, dark blue flowers. Pearl-white shaded blossoms are borne by 'Silver White'. 'Strata' has blue flowers with white calyces. 'Victoria' displays violet-blue flowers and calyces. 'White Porcelain' bears white flowers.

Salvia greggii • Autumn Sage

☼–☀ ◊
❀ Scarlet, red
↕ 4' in its native habitat; 20" as garden annual ↔ 20"–24"; plant 15"–18" apart.

Autumn sage is a native of the rocky, mountainous areas of southwest Texas throughout the Chihuahuan desert into Mexico. It is a woody perennial that's grown as an annual in colder climates. The mid-green leaves vary in shape and tend to be less than 1 inch in length and are leathery in texture and hairless to softly hairy. The ¾- to 1¼-inch-long wide-lipped flowers are produced in late summer through autumn on upright terminal racemes. In addition to attracting hummingbirds, bees, and butterflies, autumn sage makes an excellent cut flower.

Growing Tips Autumn sage prefers low humidity and loamy soil with excellent drainage. Sow seeds eight weeks before the last frost and set plants out when the ground is thoroughly warmed. Pinch throughout the long growing season to encourage bushiness and remove spent racemes often to encourage continuous bloom. Autumn sage is hardy to Zones 7 to 9.

***Salvia farinacea* 'Victoria', mealy-cup sage.**

Salvia greggii, **autumn sage.**

Companion Plants Mix autumn sage with bread seed poppy (*Papaver* 'Double Raspberry Blush'), tender, deep-pink-flowered evening primrose (*Oenothera kunthiana*), and annual mallow (*Malope trifida* 'Glacier Fruits') with red and pink shades.

Cultivars *Salvia greggii* 'Alba' displays white flowers. 'Big Pink' has larger blossoms than the species, each deep pink with a lavender tint. 'Cherry Red' is a reliable bloomer in the humid South and has proved reliable in partially shaded sites. 'Purple Haze' bears small but intensely colored violet-purple blossoms. Slightly shorter than the species, 'Purple Pastel' is charming. It is a good repeat bloomer in the fall. 'Raspberry Royal' has bright raspberry-red flowers.

Salvia leucantha • Mexican Bush Sage

☼ ◌

❀ White, rarely purple

↕ 24"–48" ↔ 24" in one season; 3'–6' over several years; plant 15"–18" apart.

This is a beautifully striking tall, evergreen subshrub hailing from central and eastern Mexico southward to tropical Central America, which is grown as an annual in colder areas. It has white downy stems when young, and the 6-inch-long medium-green lance-shaped leaves are wrinkled above and downy beneath. From late summer on it produces terminal racemes with ½- to ¾-inch flowers that emerge from bell-shaped downy purple calyces. As with other *Salvia* species, it is extremely attractive to wildlife.

Growing Tips Mexican bush sage prefers well-drained ordinary garden soil. Start seeds indoors six to eight weeks before the last frost date. Remove spent inflorescences to encourage new racemes. Hardy to Zones 10 to 11.

Companion Plants Combine Mexican bush sage with pink-flowered rosemary (*Rosmarinus* 'Roseus'), French lavender (*Lavendula stoechas*), and carmine-rose California poppy (*Eschscholzia* 'Carmine King').

Cultivars *Salvia leucantha* 'Midnight' has deep-violet flowers and calyces. It is quite common in cultivation in the western United States.

Salvia mexicana • Mexican Sage

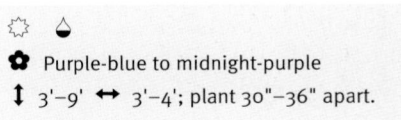

☼ ◌

❀ Purple-blue to midnight-purple

↕ 3'–9' ↔ 3'–4'; plant 30"–36" apart.

Mexican sage can be found growing wild in many areas throughout central Mexico. The foliage of this sage is quite inconsistent in size and color—some plants have mid-green, glabrous leaves while others have gray-green foliage with short hairs covering the surface. Beginning in late summer, the long racemes of flowers are produced until the plant is stopped by frost. As a nectar source, the flowers are highly attractive to butterflies, bees, and hummingbirds.

The flowering branches are quite beautiful as cut flowers.

Growing Tips Start Mexican sage from seed indoors eight weeks before the last frost date and plant it out in a well-drained spot when the soil is thoroughly warmed. Plants need support in an exposed site. Remove spent inflorescences to encourage new blooms. Take cuttings in summer. It is hardy to Zone 9.

Companion Plants Play up the chartreuse and midnight-purple flowers with chartreuse-flowered *Zinnia* 'Double Envy', *Nicotiana* 'Limelight', or deep ocean-blue prairie gentian (*Eustoma* 'The Blue Rose').

Cultivars *Salvia mexicana* 'Limelight' bears large chartreuse-green calyces and vibrant violet-blue flowers. 'Lollie Jackson' has larger flowers than the species and is considered compact at 4 feet tall. 'Ocampo' is upright in growth habit and can reach 7 feet in height.

Salvia viridis • **Red-Topped Sage**

☼ ◐-◆
◉ Pink, purple, or white bracts
↕ 12"–24" ↔ 9"–12"; plant 10" apart.

In the wild, this unusual little sage occurs in a region that stretches from the Mediterranean eastward into Crimea and Iran. It is an erect, bushy annual with ovate to oblong notched, hairy medium-green leaves to 2 inches long. In summer, it bears terminal spikes of insignificant whorled flowers, with each floret enclosed in two very showy bracts to 1½ inches long, with darker venation. It makes an excellent fresh-cut or dried flower.

Growing Tips Good drainage and friable soil are all red-topped sage requires. Sow seeds eight weeks before the last frost date or sow directly in the garden when the soil has thoroughly warmed—to at least 70°F. The seedlings are stout and hardy and transplant easily. In areas with mild winters, volunteer seedlings are probable. Remove spent inflorescences to encourage repeat blooming.

Companion Plants The brightly colored bracts of the red-topped sage are offset remarkably well by silver-leafed plants such as licorice plant (*Helichrysum petiolare*), *Plectranthus argentatus,* or dusty miller (*Senecio cineraria* 'Silver Dust'). Alternatively, combine it with *Verbena* 'Quartz Blue', which has medium blue, white-eyed florets, or *V.* 'Romance Purple', which displays deep purple, white-eyed florets.

Cultivars *Salvia viridis* 'Claryssa' is a compact 16 inches tall and well branched, with bracts in rose-pink, blue, purple, or white. It is available in single colors as well. 'Oxford Blue' is shorter, at 12 inches, and displays violet-blue bracts. 'Pink Sundae' has bright carmine-pink bracts, and the bracts of 'White Swan' are white with green veins.

Salvia viridis **'Claryssa', red-topped sage.**

More Recommendations

Many of the annuals mentioned elsewhere in this volume are versatile beauties that can play many roles in the garden. Following are selected annuals that provide nectar for butterflies and hummingbirds, hardy annuals that can tolerate light frost and in some cases even a little snow, and cool-season annuals that can be grown in fall and winter in warm-winter areas of the deep South and West.

Nectar Plants for Butterflies, Hummingbirds, and Bees

Agastache species Giant hyssops, page 49
Ammi majus Bishop's weed, page 50
Antirrhinum majus Common snapdragon, page 50
Cleome hassleriana Spider flower, page 77
Consolida ajacis Larkspur, page 17
Coreopsis tinctoria Golden coreopsis, page 12
Cosmos bipinnatus Cosmos, page 12
Fuchsia species Fuchsias, page 62
Impatiens species Impatiens, page 64–65
Ipomoea lobata Spanish flag, page 46
Ipomoea × multifida Cardinal climber, page 47
Lathyrus odoratus Sweet pea, page 57
Limonium sinuatum 'Art Shades' statice, page 20
Mandevilla species Mandevilla vines, page 73
Matthiola longipetala Night-scented stock, page 38
Mirabilis jalapa Four-o'-clock, page 38

Nicotiana langsdorffii Flowering tobacco, page 59
Passiflora coccinea Passionflower, page 74
Rudbeckia 'Sunset' Black-eyed susan, page 14

A Monarch butterfly sips nectar on a blossom of *Ipomoea lobata*, Spanish flag.

Clarkia amoena, satin flower.

Salvia coccinea Scarlet sage, page 84
Salvia greggii Autumn sage, page 86
Salvia leucantha Mexican bush sage,
    page 87
Salvia mexicana Mexican sage, page 87
Scabiosa atropurpurea Pincushion flower,
    page 80
Tithonia rotundifolia, Mexican sunflower,
    page 16
Verbena bonariensis Verbena bo, page 82
Zinnia angustifolia, Thread-leaf zinnia,
    page 16

Hardy Annuals

Ammi majus Bishop's weed, page 50
Beta vulgaris Swiss chard, page 25
Brassica oleracea var. *acephala* Kale, page 26
Briza maxima Quaking grass, page 17
Calendula officinalis Pot marigold, page 11
Clarkia amoena Satin flower, page 51
Consolida ajacis Larkspur, page 17
Coreopsis tinctoria Golden coreopsis, page 12
Cynara scolymus Globe artichoke, page 32
Euphorbia marginata Snow-on-the-
    mountain, page 33
Lathyrus odoratus Sweet pea, page 57

Linaria maroccana Toadflax, page 58
Malope trifida Annual mallow, page 58
Matthiola longipetala Night-scented stock,
    page 38
Papaver nudicaule Iceland poppy, page 60
Salvia viridis Red-topped sage, page 88
Scabiosa atropurpurea Pincushion flower,
    page 80

Cool-Season Annuals for the Deep South and West

Antirrhinum majus Common snapdragon,
    page 50
Beta vulgaris Swiss chard, page 25
Brassica oleracea var. *acephala* Kale, page 26
Calendula officinalis Pot marigold, page 11
Clarkia amoena Satin flower, page 51
Cynara scolymus Globe artichoke, page 32
Lathyrus odoratus Sweet pea, page 57
Linaria maroccana Toadflax, page 58
Matthiola longipetala Night-scented stock,
    page 38
Mauranthemum paludosum, page 14
Papaver nudicaule Iceland poppy, page 60
Petroselinum crispum Parsley, page 28
Salvia viridis Red-topped sage, page 88

Growing Basics

Buying Annuals

Picking out bedding plants at the local garden center is quick and easy. And at the best nurseries the choice of annuals expands every year. However, you will still have to grow from seed to get the widest selection; fortunately, annuals are some of the easiest plants to start from seed (see "A Step-by-Step Guide to Propagation," page 96).

When shopping for plants, there are a few things to keep in mind: Make sure the plants are robust and healthy but not too mature. Yellowed, wilted foliage and leggy growth are signs of overcrowded growing conditions, inadequate nutrition, and/or improper watering practices. Avoid annuals in full bloom unless you are intentionally seeking mature plants for midsummer planting. When you put blooming plants in the ground, they are slow to produce new roots and often grow poorly. Although a few open flowers will confirm the desired color—mislabeling is the bane of color coordination—it's best to remove all the flowers *and* buds when you plant. This encourages strong root and shoot production, which in turn produces masses of flowers.

Transplanting

When you are ready to transplant nursery-grown annuals or home-grown seedlings, spread a generous, two-inch layer of compost and some organic fertilizer over the planting area. These will get worked into the soil as you plant. Using a trowel, dig planting holes, spacing them according to the instructions in the "Encyclopedia of

Annuals" beginning on page 9, or on the plant labels or seed packets. It may seem like a lot of room at first, but the plants will fill in rapidly.

To remove the plants from their containers, put one hand, palm down, over the top of the pot and carefully turn it upside down. With your other hand, tap the pot to loosen the plant, then lift it off. Annuals grown in peat pots can simply be placed into the hole, pot and all.

If the roots have formed a tight mat, it will be difficult for them to grow out into the surrounding soil. Take a sharp knife and cut from the top of one side down, across the bottom, and up the other side. New roots will form along the cut line and spread out into the soil.

When you've set out all the plants, water them well, then work the soil back around the plants. The rootballs should be at the same depth as they were in their containers. Weak and leggy plants can be planted somewhat deeper, to the depth of their lowest leaves.

Watering

The best way to keep your annuals moist is to mulch. Immediately after planting, cover the soil with a two-inch layer of organic material such as shredded leaves or bark. This will also minimize weed problems. Organic mulches should not be applied

---

Degrees of Sun and Shade

Following are the terms commonly used to describe the light requirements of garden plants. Keep in mind that the precise amount of sunshine required for any particular plant will vary, depending on the region. For example, annuals listed as "sun loving" may tolerate full sun in cool climates but would burn up in midsummer in hot, dry areas of the West and Southwest unless planted in daylong light shade or at least afternoon shade.

FULL SUN: A minimum of 10 to 12 hours a day of direct sun in midsummer. What do you do when you want to grow an annual labeled "full sun" but your flower bed gets only 6 to 8 hours of sun a day? Generally, you should go ahead and plant it because chances are it will do well.

LIGHT SHADE: Bright to full sun for roughly half the day.

PARTIAL SHADE, PARTIAL SUN: Bright light or sunshine for roughly half the day.

FULL SHADE: The sun is obstructed for most of the day.

around plants that require dry soil. Mulches will also prevent annuals from self-sowing, so you may want to leave some mulch-free spots around plants you would like to seed around.

In most climates, mulching will almost eliminate the need for supplemental water, especially if you have selected plants with moderate moisture requirements. When irrigation is necessary, use soaker hoses in garden beds and drip irrigation for container plantings. These not only conserve water but also keep the leaves dry, minimizing disease problems.

Fertilizing

If you make a habit of adding a layer of compost to your flower beds annually and add a bit of fertilizer at planting time, your annuals won't require much additional fertilization. If some of your plants begin to look tired as summer wears on, developing yellow leaves or failing to bloom, you can spot-fertilize with a foliar spray. Two organic choices are liquid seaweed or fish emulsion. Foliar sprays are widely available at garden centers. Use according to the directions on the label and your plants will perk up right away.

Pinching, Disbudding, and Deadheading

Three routine gardening chores—pinching, disbudding, and deadheading—are the secret to abundant blooms. They can mean the difference between sensational annuals and ho-hum ones. While they are important in the care of biennials and perennials and even some shrubs, they are absolutely crucial for a successful floriferous planting of annuals.

Pinching. Pinching is the process of using the thumb and forefinger to pinch off (hence the name) a plant's growing tip or tips. Pinching promotes the development of side branches, making an annual more compact and bushy. Increasing the number of branches in turn makes it possible for the plant to

If you regularly remove the flower spikes of annuals grown for their foliage, such as coleus, the plants will spend more energy on growing leaves.

produce more flowers. Annuals that benefit from pinching include such foliage plants as coleus (*Solenostemon*), *Ruellia,* and *Alternathera,* and such flowering favorites as zinnias, snapdragons, fuchsias, and salvias. A couple of pinchings several weeks apart will usually suffice.

Disbudding. Many annuals, such as sunflowers, dahlias, and strawflowers, produce one large flower subtended by one or more smaller ones. The removal of the smaller flowers allows the remaining bud to form a larger, stronger blossom. Conversely, allowing all of the buds to open creates a bouquetlike cluster of smaller flowers. In the case of annuals that bear flowers on spikes, such as stock, larkspur, and salvia, the side spikes can be removed to enhance the size of the primary spike, or they may be allowed to mature, creating a tiered effect.

To encourage abundant blooms, remove spent flower heads of annuals, such as marigolds, every week.

Annuals grown for their foliage, such as coleus, require constant attention. Remove their unsightly, energy-consuming flower spikes as they develop in order to keep the plants in top form.

Deadheading. All spent flowers should be removed on a weekly basis. If I may be permitted to anthropomorphize for a moment, when annuals set their seed, they feel their life's work has been accomplished, and flower production decreases or halts altogether. Deadheading—removing spent flowers—inhibits seed formation and encourages continued flower production.

Opposite: Coleus cultivars mingle with red cabbage, kale, fennel, and perennial black-eyed susan.

A Step-by-Step Guide to Propagation

Propagation, the practice of making more plants, can be accomplished in several ways. Since unusual plants are sometimes expensive or hard to find, it's handy to know how to start your own. Once you can propagate the plants you want, there's very little to stand in the way of your growing uncommon beauties. The following is an introduction to propagation from seed, from cuttings, and by division.

Seeds

Many of the annuals discussed in this handbook are easy to grow from seed, which is worth trying for several reasons. First, the feeling of satisfaction is enormous. You can look at your garden and say to yourself, "I did this, from start to finish." Second, it's much cheaper to buy seed than to buy small plants. A package of seeds usually costs less than two dollars, even for exotic varieties. And quite a few unusual plants are not easy to find, whereas the seeds tend to be more readily available.

Read the Seed Packet. Most seed packets provide good information, so be sure you read their planting instructions before proceeding.

Moisten the Mix. Next, purchase sterile soilless seed-starting mix and pour it into a large bucket, add water, and stir. The mix should be moist enough to hold a clump when you squeeze it but not so wet that water drips out of the clump when you squeeze. Fill your flat (or large pot) with soil and firm it down. The soil level should reach to half an inch below the edge of the flat.

Sow the Seeds. Most seeds do not require light to germinate, so they should be

The basic steps of seed starting, clockwise from top left: Pour soilless mix into a bucket, add water, and stir. The mix should be moist enough to hold in a clump when you squeeze it. Fill a seed-starting flat with the moistened mix, tamp it down, and plant the seeds. Be sure to keep the emerging seedlings moist. To hold in humidity, cover the flat with a see-through lid until the seedlings are so tall that they nearly bump up against it.

covered with a thin layer of the soilless medium. A good general rule is that a seed should be buried as deep as it is large. For example, the very small seeds of *Portulaca grandiflora* need to be covered by only a very thin layer of the mix. If you're planting morning glory (*Ipomoea alba*), a seed the size of a kernel of corn, cover with about a quarter inch of mix.

If seeds are large, poke holes in the seed-starting mix with the end of a pencil. Make the holes about half an inch deep and space them two inches apart. Place a seed in each hole and press the mix over the seed with your finger. If the seeds are small, take a ruler and press a long trench, about a quarter-inch deep, into the mix. Scatter the seeds into the trench, then press the mix over the seeds.

If your seeds require light to germinate, like the seeds of stock (*Matthiola longipetala*) or flowering tobacco (*Nicotiana*), don't cover the seeds with any mix. Small seeds can be sown in a trench but should not be covered. Large seeds can be pressed into the top of the mix and left uncovered.

If you're sowing seeds in individual pots, you must decide how many seeds to plant per pot. If seeds are large, try one or two per pot; if they're small, try more.

Seed-Starting Tools

Here's what you'll need to get started: a lightweight sterile seed-starting mix; a few flats or large, shallow pots; some small biodegradable pots (no larger than two inches in diameter); and your seeds.

SEED-STARTING MIX. Garden soil and many potting-soil mixes are too heavy for starting seeds. They retain so much moisture that the seeds can rot. A lightweight seed-starting mix is usually soilless and will keep seeds moist but not too wet.

FLATS. A flat is a rectangular pan with drainage holes in the bottom that can be used for starting lots of seeds at once. It's usually about two or three inches deep. Start one kind of seed per flat, because different seeds have different cultural requirements. If you don't have a flat, you can use a large, shallow pot. This will be the germination site only. Once your seeds have one or two sets of true leaves, you'll move them up to larger pots or transplant them outdoors.

INDIVIDUAL BIODEGRADABLE POTS. Some plants are finicky about being transplanted; they don't like having their roots disturbed. For these, start the seeds in individual biodegradable pots. When seedlings are ready, you can plant the entire pot in the garden with no root disturbance whatsoever.

After planting your seeds, mist the soil surface with water to settle the seeds in place. To keep the humidity high, cover the flat or pot with a piece of plastic wrap or glass, or enclose the entire flat in a clear dry-cleaning bag.

You may want to invest in an inexpensive germination/propagation unit, which includes a clear plastic cover for keeping ambient humidity high. Once seeds have sprouted and top growth is approaching the plastic, it's time to remove the dome and think about transplanting. Some propagation setups include an insulated base and heat mat, which is especially handy for starting seeds of plants that require extra warmth and for rooting cuttings.

Provide Moisture. Your seed packet should tell you how much time the seeds need to germinate. During this time it's important to keep the starting mix moist but not wet; high humidity is also helpful. Check the surface of your mix every day, and if the top feels dry to the touch, water it. Since you don't want to disturb the seeds, be sure to water gently. Try breaking the force of the water by pouring it through your fingers or by using a rose attached to your watering can.

Opposite: For the widest selection, it's best to start annuals from seed. Fortunately, they are some of the easiest plants to grow.

ETTE

ROTHERS

AINE

Miss

SP

Seed
Annual

F. S.
S
AND

RANUNCULUS
GIANT MIXED

SWEET WILLIAM
FANCY MIXED ROYAL
PRICE
10¢

DIGITAL
FANCY MIXED

GLOSSIS
MIXED

QUALITY

Transplant the Seedlings. The first leaf (or pair of leaves) to emerge is called the cotelydon, which means seed leaf. This is not a true leaf, but was once contained inside the seed as a source of nutrition for the young plant. The next leaves to emerge are true leaves. When seedlings have two sets of true leaves, they are ready to be transplanted, either into the garden or into larger pots, where their roots can grow without becoming entangled with those of other plants.

If you're moving plants from a flat into individual pots, be sure not to use pots that are too large. A pot two inches in diameter is large enough for most seedlings. Lift the seedling out of the flat with a spoon, being careful to disturb the roots as little as possible. Hold the seedling by a leaf, never by its stem. If you damage a leaf, the plant can grow another. If you damage the stem, you kill the plant.

Plant Outdoors. Once the risk of frost in your area has passed, it's time to plant your seedlings outside. Transplant seedlings at the same level at which they were originally planted. Do not expose the roots or bury the stem. Remember, your seedlings will grow a lot, so give them room. In most cases, crowded plants don't get the nutrition or air circulation they need and will not grow to their full potential. Water in your new seedlings and give their roots a few weeks to establish themselves before their first feeding.

Sowing Seed Outdoors

Sowing outdoors is the best way to grow annuals that don't like to be transplanted, and also those that grow quickly from seed. It's also a good way to establish annuals around fragile bulbs and dormant perennials. Keep in mind, though, that annuals sown directly outdoors will take longer to flower than those set out as young plants.

The right time to sow varies by climate. Usually, annuals are sown in early spring, and the seeds germinate when conditions are right. In Zones 6 and higher, and in colder areas where there is good snow cover in winter, many annuals can be sown in the fall and will germinate the following spring. In very mild climates, Zones 9 to 11, cool-loving annuals can also be sown in late summer or early fall for autumn and winter bloom.

If you're sowing seeds in a new flower bed, start by amending the soil with about two inches of compost and some organic fertilizer. Rake these lightly into the soil, sow the seeds, and water. If the seeds need to be covered, rake the spot lightly. For seeds that don't need to be covered, lightly press the soil with the flat end of a metal rake or other blunt tool after sowing, then water.

Cuttings

Propagation by cuttings is another way to increase your plant collection. It's also a good way to keep plants over the winter if you don't have room indoors for the entire plant. Cuttings only work for tender perennials grown as annuals. They will not work for true annuals—these need to be propagated from seed. Tropical perennials like coleus (*Solenostemon*), *Hoya, Mandevilla*, and *Abutilon* are easy to grow from cuttings. You'll need rooting hormone (liquid or powder), a lightweight potting mix, and some small pots (two to four inches in diameter).

Prepare the Potting Mix. Begin by moistening the potting mix and filling your pots as you did for starting seed. Once again, soilless mix should be firmed down and reach to half an inch below the edge of the pot. Taking a pencil, poke one hole into the soil for each cutting you'll start. Poke the hole two to three inches deep.

Prepare the Cutting. Next, take a six-inch cutting from the end of your plant, making the cut just above a node (where the leaves branch out from the stem). Pinch out the growing tip of the plant and remove the bottom two leaves from the stem. Dip the bottom of the cutting into rooting hormone so that it covers the stem up to the node where the leaves were removed. Tap off excess hormone and stick the coated end of the cutting in the potting mix. Firm the mix around the cuttings and water them in.

If you've made cuttings to overwinter some of your favorites, limit their size by growing them in small pots and pinching the growing tips.

Provide Humidity. Cuttings will grow roots along the stem where you've applied the hormone. Because they have no root systems with which to transport water, cuttings

Tender Perennials That Are Easy to Propagate From Cuttings

Cuttings of most plants are best taken anytime during the growing season. The warmer temperatures and higher light levels during this time make the plants grow faster, which speeds the rooting process.

Agastache species Giant hyssops, page 49

Begonia hybrids Cane-stemmed group, page 62

Breynia nivosa 'Roseopicta' Snowbush, page 31

Datura inoxia Angel's trumpet, page 36

Fuchsia species and cultivars Fuchsias, page 62

Hoya carnosa Wax plant, page 72

Ipomoea batatas Sweet-potato vine, page 45

Melianthus major Honey flower, page 34

Passiflora species Passionflower, page 74

Saccharum officinarum 'Violaceum' Purple sugarcane, page 28

Salvia mexicana Mexican sage, page 87

need supplemental humidity while they're rooting. By misting the cuttings and enclosing them in clear plastic to create a greenhouse effect, you will improve your chances of success. Placing the cuttings on top of a heat mat can further speed the rooting process.

Transplant the Cutting. When you see new top growth, you'll know roots have established well enough to allow transplanting.

Division

Many perennials are propagated by division, which simply means digging up a large plant and splitting the root system (with top growth attached) into pieces. This technique works for many nonhardy perennials that are grown as annuals. Four-o'-clock (*Mirabilis jalapa*) is a tender perennial that can be overwintered by digging up and cleaning off the roots after the first frost. Roots should be put in a plastic bag or pot of soil and kept in the dark at temperatures between 35°F to 40°F. Check them periodically to make sure they don't shrivel up or dry out. You may need to water them once or twice during the winter. In spring, roots can be divided by cutting them into pieces with a pruner. Make sure each piece includes at least two nodes. Then pot, water, and move the divisions into the light to restart top growth.

For More Information

Annuals and Biennials
Roger Phillips and Martyn Rix
Firefly Books, 2002

Annuals and Bulbs
Rob Proctor, with Nancy J. Ondra
Rodale Press, 1995

Annuals for Connoisseurs
Wayne Winterrowd
Prentice Hall, 1992

Annuals for Every Purpose
Larry Hodgson
Rodale Press, 2001

The Annual Garden
Peter Loewer
Rodale Press, 1988

Annuals With Style
Michael A. Ruggiero and
Tom Christopher
Taunton Press, 2000

*Annuals: Yearly Classics for the
Contemporary Garden*
Rob Proctor
HarperCollins, 1991

*Armitage's Manual of Annuals,
Biennials, and Half-Hardy Perennials*
Allan M. Armitage
Timber Press, 2001

A Book of Salvias
Betsy Clebsch
Timber Press, 1997

The Bountiful Container
Rose Marie Nichols McGee and
Maggie Stuckey
Workman, 2002

Discovering Annuals
Graham Rice
Timber Press, 1999

Pansies
Scott D. Appell
Friedman/Fairfax, 1999

*Poppies: The Poppy Family in the Wild
and in Cultivation*
Christopher Grey-Wilson
Timber Press, revised edition, 2000

Specialty Cut Flowers
Allan M. Armitage
Varsity Press/Timber Press, 1993

Mail-Order Sources

Abundant Life Seed Foundation
P.O. Box 772
Port Townsend, WA 98358
360-385-5660
www.abundantlifeseed.org

Baker Creek Heirloom Seeds
2278 Baker Creek Road
Mansfield, MO 65704
417-924-8917
www.rareseeds.com

Color Farm Coleus Catalog
1604 West Richway Drive
Albert Lea, MN 56007
(no phone orders or web site)

The Cook's Garden
P.O. Box 535
Londonderry, VT 05148
800-457-9703
www.cooksgarden.com

High Country Gardens
2902 Rufina Street
Santa Fe, NM 87507
800-925-9387
www.highcountrygardens.com

J.L. Hudson, Seedsman
Star Route 2, Box 337
La Honda, CA 94020
www.jlhudsonseeds.net

Johnny's Selected Seeds
184 Foss Hill Road
Albion, ME 04910
207-437-9294
www.johnnyseeds.com

Nichols Garden Nursery
1190 Old Salem Road NE
Albany, OR 97321
800-422-3985
www.nicholsgardennursery.com

Seeds of Change
P.O. Box 15700
Santa Fe, NM 87506
888-762-7333
www.seedsofchange.com

Select Seeds Antique Flowers
180 Stickney Hill Road
Union, CT 06076
860-684-9310
www.selectseeds.com

Thompson & Morgan Seedsmen
P.O. Box 1308
Jackson, NJ 08527
800-274-7333
www.thompsonandmorgan.com

Well-Sweep Herb Farm
205 Mount Bethel Road
Port Murray, NJ 07865
908-852-5390
www.wellsweep.com

Contributors

SCOTT D. APPELL has written four books, *Pansies, Lilies, Tulips,* and *Orchids.* In addition, he is the editor of Brooklyn Botanic Garden handbooks *Landscaping Indoors* (2000) and *The Potted Garden* (2001). He is director of horticulture at the St. George Village Botanical Garden in St. Croix, U.S. Virgin Islands; a former member of the Publications Committee of the Pennsylvania Horticultural Society; and a board member of the American Violet Society. His private consultation company is called The Green Man™.

He is the editor of *Annuals for Every Garden,* for which he wrote the chapters "Mad About Annuals" and "Growing Basics" as well as its encyclopedia articles "Long-Lasting Flowers," "Edible Annuals," "Annuals With Fabulous Foliage," "Morning Glories and Their Relatives," "Annuals for Picking," "Annuals for Shade," and "Sensational Salvias."

ROSE G. EDINGER is an award-winning, freelance floral designer. She owned Aalsmeer Flower Market in New York and has 20 years of experience in the floral industry. She specializes in thematic design work and has decorated events throughout the New York region and abroad. She is currently an instructor in the floral-design certificate programs at the Horticultural Society of New York and at Brooklyn Botanic Garden and has lectured at numerous garden-club events.

She wrote the sidebar "Care of Fresh-Cut Annuals From the Garden," which appears on page 52.

Contributors, *continued*

ELLEN ZACHOS is a Harvard graduate and received her Certificate in Horticulture from The New York Botanical Garden. She specializes in tropical plants and has restored several greenhouses in the New York City area, which she now maintains for her clients. Her company, Acme Plant Stuff, installs and maintains commercial and residential interior and exterior gardens in New York City.

She is the author of this handbook's chapter "A Step-by-Step Guide to Propagation" as well as the encyclopedia articles "Delightful Daisies," "Evening Bloomers," "Tender Tropicals," and "Drought-Tolerant Bloomers."

Illustration
EMMA SKURNICK page 7

Photos
DAVID CAVAGNARO cover, pages 2, 4, 12, 13, 15, 18, 23, 26, 27, 30, 33, 34, 35, 37, 39, 46, 47, 48, 50, 51, 56, 57, 59, 60, 63, 65, 66, 70, 73, 74, 80, 81, 82, 83, 85, 87, 88, 89, 93, 94, 95, 99

ALAN & LINDA DETRICK pages 8, 16, 40, 52, 79, 86

MAGGIE OSTER pages 10, 54

NEIL SODERSTROM pages 19, 44, 97

DEREK FELL pages 20, 22, 24, 36, 38, 40, 64, 67, 72, 90

JERRY PAVIA pages 29, 32, 43, 47, 55, 62, 68, 71, 75, 77, 78, 84

Index

A

Abelmoschus esculentus, 23
   'Burgundy', 23
   'Cajun Delight', 23
   'Cowhorn', 23
Abutilon
   × *hybridum,* 69
   megapotamicum, 69
   pictum, 69
Agastache, 49, 89, 102
   'Apricot Sprite', 49
   cana, 49
   'Pink Panther', 49
Amaranthus
   caudatus, 69–70
   tricolor, 70
Ammi
   majus, 50, 89, 90
   majus 'Green Mist', 50
   visnaga, 50
Angel's Trumpet, 36–37, 102
Annuals
   aster family, 11–16
   care of, 91–94
   categories of, 5–8
   for cutting, 49–60
   for drying, 17–22
   drought-tolerant, 76–81
   edible, 23–30

evening bloomers, 36–41
for foliage, 31–35
hardy, 6, 90
information sources, 103
mail-order sources, 104
nectar, 89–90
overwintering, 8
self-seeding, 101
for shade, 61–67
for South and West, 90
tropicals, 68–75
versatility of, 5
See also Propagation;
specific names
Antirrhinum majus, 6, 7,
   50–51, 89, 90
Argyreia nervosa, 42, 43
Aster family, 11–16

B

Baby's Breath, 56–57
Bacopa cordata, 61
   'Blue Showers', 61
   'Gold & Pearl', 61
   'Snowstorm', 61
Banana, Ornamental, 73–74
Basella alba, 25
   'Rubra', 25
Bees, nectar plants for, 89–90

Begonia
   Cane-Stemmed, 62, 102
   Rex-Begonia Vine, 31–32
Bells-of-Ireland, 21
Beta vulgaris 25, 90
   'Bright Lights', 25
   'Rainbow', 25
   'Ruby Red', 25
Bishop's Weed, 50
Black-Eyed Susan, 14, 89
Bougainvillea
   glabra, 76
   spectabilis, 76
Bracteantha bracteata, 11
   'Bronze Gold', 11
   'Pink', 11
Brassica oleracea var. *acephala*,
   26, 90
Breynia nivosa
   'Roseopicta', 31, 102
Briza maxima 'Rubra', 17, 90
Burning Love, 78
Butterfly plants, 89–90

C

Calabash Vine, 37–38
Calendula officinalis, 11–12,
   90, 101
   'Pacific Beauty', 12

Capsicum annuum, 26–27
   'Fatali', 27
   'Filus Blue', 27
   'Little Elf', 27
Cardinal Climber, 47, 89
Carmel Daisy, 22
Cassava, Variegated, 28
Castor Bean, 35
Catchfly, 41
Celosia argentea
   Cristata group, 70, 71
   Plumosa group, 70, 71
Chard, 25, 90
Chrysanthemum, 14
Cissus discolor, 31–32
Clarkia amoena, 51, 90
Claytonia, 66
Cleome hassleriana, 77, 89, 101
   'Queen Series', 77
Cockscomb, 70–71
Codiaeum variegatum
   var. *pictum*, 71–72
   'Carrierei', 72
Coleus, 6, 7, 94
Colocasia 'Black Magic', 7
Composite family, 11–16
Consolida ajacis, 17–18, 89, 90
   'Dwarf Hyacinth', 18
   'Earl Grey', 18
   'Frosted Skies', 18
Convolvulus
   cneorum, 42, 43–44
   tricolor, 44
Coreopsis tinctoria (Golden),
   12, 89, 90, 101
Cosmos
   bipinnatus, 12–13, 89, 101
   sulphureus, 13
Cotton
   Levant, 20
   Sea Island, 20
Croton, 71–72
Cryptanthus

bivattatus, 72
fosteranus, 72
Curry Plant, 77–78
Cut flowers
   care of, 52–53
   commonly used, 7
   harvesting, 52
   preservative for, 53
   varieties of, 49–60
Cuttings, propagation by,
   101–2
Cynara scolymus, 32, 90
   'Green Globe', 32
   'Imperial Star', 32
Cypress vine, 37

D

Dahlia, 6, 7, 94
Daisy
   aster family, 11–16
   Carmel, 22
   Transvaal (Gerbera), 54, 56
Datura
   inoxia, 36–37, 102
   metel, 37
Deadheading, 94
Devil's Claw, 21
Diamond Flower, 65–66
Disbudding, 94
Division, propagation by, 102
Drying, annuals for, 17–22
Drought-tolerant plants,
   76–81
Dusty Miller, 6

E

Earth Star, 72
Edible annuals, 23–30
Eggplant, 29–30
Ensete ventricosum
   'Maurelii', 74
Eschscholzia californica, 60
Euphorbia heterophylla, 33

marginata, 33, 90, 101
pulcherrima, 33
Eustoma grandiflorum, 54
   'Aloha Deep Red', 54
   'Double Eagle Mixed', 54
   'Mermaid Extra Dwarf', 54
Evening-flowering plants,
   36–41
Evolvulus pilosus, 45
   'Blue Daze', 45

F

Feather Grass, 78–79
Felicia amelloides, 13
   'Montrosa', 13
Fertilizing, 93
Flats, 98
Flax
   New Zealand, 79
Foliage plants, 31–35
Fountain Grass, 78–79
Four-o'-Clock, 38–39, 89, 102
Fuchsia, 62–63, 89, 94, 102
Furcraea foetida 'Mediopicta',
   7, 8

G

Gentian, Prairie, 54
Geranium, Jungle, 78
Gerbera jamesonii, 54, 56
   'California Giants', 56
   'Dwarf Pandora Mixed', 56
   'Rainbow Mixed', 56
Globe Amaranth, 18
Globe Artichoke, 32, 90
Gomphrena
   globosa, 18
   haageana, 18
Gossypium
   barbadense, 20
   herbaceum 'Nigra', 20
Gourd Vine, 37–38
Grasses

Feather, 78–79
Fountain, 78–79
Quaking, Red, 17, 90
Rice, Purple-Leafed, 34
Gypsophila elegans, 56–57

H

Half-hardy annuals, 6
Hardy annuals, 6, 90
Hare's-Tail Grass, 57
Harvesting, 17, 52
Helichrysum petiolare, 6, 7, 77–78
Honey Flower, 34, 102
Hot Pepper, 26–27
Hoya
  australis, 73
  carnosa, 72–73, 102
  lacunosa, 73
Hummingbird plants, 89–90
Hyssop, Water, 61
Hyssops, Giant, 49, 102

I

Immortelle, 22
Impatiens, 89
  'African Queen', 64
  auricoma, 64
  niamniamensis 'Congo Cockatoo', 65
  tinctoria, 65
  walleriana, 64
Ionopsidium acaule, 65–66, 101
Ipomoea
  alba, 37, 97
  batatas, 7, 42, 45–46, 102
  lobata, 46, 89
  × *multifida*, 47, 89
  nil, 47
  quamoclit, 37, 47
  tricolor, 48
Ixora
  casei, 78

chinensis, 78
coccinea, 78
hookeri, 78

J

Joseph's Coat, 70

K

Kale, 26, 90

L

Lagenaria siceraria, 37–38
Lagurus ovatus, 57
Larkspur, 17–18, 89, 90, 94
Lathyrus odoratus, 57–58, 89, 90
  'Early Multiflora', 58
Leucanthemum
  multicaule, 14
  paludosum, 14
Licorice Plant, 6, 7, 77–78
Light requirements, 92
Limonium sinuatum
  'Art Shades', 20–21, 89
  'Forever Gold', 21
  'Petite Bouquet', 21
Linaria maroccana, 58, 90
  'Fairy Bouquet', 58
  'Northern Lights', 58
Long-lasting flowers, 17–22
Love-Lies-Bleeding, 69–70
Luffa cylindrica, 38

M

Mail-order sources, 104
Mallow, Annual, 58–59, 90, 101
Malope trifida, 58–59, 90, 101
  'Glacier Fruits', 59
  'Vulcan', 59
  'White Queen', 59
Mandevilla, 73, 89
  × *amabilis*, 73

boliviensis, 73
splendens, 73
Manihot esculenta 'Variegata', 28
Maple, Flowering, 69
Marguerite, Blue, 13
Marigold, 15–16
  Pot, 11–12, 90, 101
Martynia annua, 21
Matthiola
  incana, 38
  longipetala, 38, 89, 90, 97
Mauranthemum paludosum, 14, 90, 101
Mauritius Hemp, 7, 8
Melianthus
  cosmosus, 34
  major, 34, 102
  villosus, 34
Melon Pear, 30
Miner's Lettuce, 66
Mirabilis jalapa, 38–39, 89, 102
  'Broken Colors', 39
Moluccella laevis, 21
Montia perfoliata, 66
Moonflower, 37
Morning Glory, 47, 48, 97
  Dwarf, 44
  growing tips, 42–43
  Woolly, 43
Moss Rose, 80
Mulching, 92–93
Musa
  acuminata 'Super Dwarf', 74
  'Zebrina', 73–74

N

Nectar plants, 89–90
Nicotiana, 97
  alata, 39–40
  langsdorffii, 40, 59–60, 89

× *sanderae*, 40

sylvestris, 40

Night-blooming plants, 36–41

Nymphaea

   caerulea, 41

   lotus, 40–41

   'Red Flare', 41

   'Sir Galahad', 41

O

Okra, Purple-Leafed, 23

Oryza sativa

   'Nigrescens', 34

   'Red Dragon', 34

Overwintering, 8, 102

P

Palm Tree Cabbage, 26

Papaver nudicaule, 60, 90

   'Champagne Bubbles', 60

   'Wonderland', 60

Parsley, 28

   Curly, 28

   Italian, 28

Passiflora, 74, 89, 102

   alata, 74

   caerulea, 74

   trifasciata, 74

Passionflower, 74, 89, 102

Pennisetum

   setaceum, 78–79

   villosum, 78–79

Pepino, 30

Pepper, Hot, 26–27

Perennials, tender, 8, 102

Perilla, 94

Petroselinum crispum, 28, 90

   var. *crispum*, 28

   var. *neapolitanum*, 28

Phlox, Night, 41

Phormium tenax, 79

Pinching, 93–94

Pincushion Flower, 80, 90

Planting, 91–92, 100

Plectranthus argentatus, 6, 7

Poppy

   California, 60

   Iceland, 60, 90

Portulaca

   grandiflora, 80, 97

   oleracea, 80

Pots, biodegradable, 98

Potting mix, 101

Preservative, cut-flower, 53

Proboscidea louisiana, 21

Propagation

   by cuttings, 101–2

   by division, 102

   by seeds, 91, 96–98, 100

   self-seeding, 101

Q

Quaking Grass, Red, 17, 90

R

Rex-Begonia Vine, 31–32

Rice, Purple-Leafed, 34

Ricinus communis, 35

   'Carmencita', 35

   'Red Spire', 35

Rose Moss, 80

Rudbeckia

   'Green Wizard', 14

   'Sunset', 14, 89

S

Saccharum officinarum

   'California Stripe', 29

   'Pele's Smoke', 29

   'Violaceum', 28–29, 102

Sage

   Andean, 85

   Autumn, 86–87, 90

   Germander, 84

   Mealy-cup, 83, 85–86

   Mexican, 87–88, 90, 102

Mexican Bush, 83, 87, 90

Red-Topped, 88, 90

Scarlet, 83, 84–85, 90

Silver, 83

Salvia, 94

   argentea, 83

   chamaedryoides, 84

   coccinea, 84–85, 90

   discolor, 85

   farinacea, 83, 85–86

   greggii, 86–87, 90

   leucantha, 83, 87, 90

   mexicana, 87–88, 90, 102

   splendens, 83

   viridis, 88, 90

Sanvitalia procumbens, 14–15

   'Sunbini', 15

Satin Flower, 51, 90

Scabiosa

   atropurpurea, 80, 90

   prolifera, 22

   stellata, 22

Seed

   self-seeding plants, 101

   sowing outdoors, 100

   starting indoors, 91, 96–98

Seedlings, transplanting, 91–92, 100

Selection criteria, 91

Senecio cineraria, 6, 7

Shade annuals, 61–67

Silene

   armeria, 41

   nutans, 41

Silverbush, 42, 43–44

Snapdragon, 6, 7, 94

   Baby, 58

   Common, 50–51, 90

Snowbush, 31, 102

Snow-on-the-Mountain, 33, 101

Soilless mix, 96, 97, 98, 101

Solanum

aethiopicum 'Aubergine du Mali', 29–30
atropurpureum, 35
melongena, 29
muricatum, 30
Solenostemon 'Palisandra', 6, 7
South, cool-season annuals for, 90
Spanish Flag, 46, 89
Spider Flower, 77, 89, 101
Spinach, Red-Stemmed Malabar, 25
Statice, 20–21, 89
Stock, Night-Scented, 38, 89, 90, 97
Strawflower, 11, 94
Sugarcane, Purple, 28–29, 102
Sunflower, 94
    Mexican, 16, 90
Sun Moss, 80
Sweet Pea, 57–58, 89
Sweet-Potato Vine, 6, 7, 42, 45–46, 102
Swiss Chard, 25

T

Tagetes
    'Lemon Gem' and 'Tangerine Gem', 15–16
    patula 'Disco Mix', 16
Taro, 6, 7
Tender annuals, 6

Tender perennials, 8
Tithonia rotundifolia, 16, 90
    'Fiesta del Sol', 16
    'Torch', 16
Toadflax, 58, 90
Tobacco, Flowering, 39–40, 59–60, 89, 97
Tools, seed-starting, 98
Torenia fournieri, 66–67
Transplanting
    cuttings, 102
    outdoors, 91–92, 100
    into pots, 100
Tropical plants, 69–75
True annuals, 6
Tuberous plants, 6

U

Unicorn Plant, 21

V

Vegetables, 23–30
Verbena
    bonariensis (Verbena Bo), 82, 90, 101
    canadensis, 82
Violet Cress, 65–66, 101

W

Watering, 92–93, 98
Water-Lily, Egyptian, 40–41
Wax Plant, 72–73, 102

West, cool-season annuals for, 90
Wishbone Flower, 66–67

X

Xeranthemum
    annuum, 22
    annuum 'Snow Lady', 22
    cylindraceum 'Lilac Star', 22

Z

Zaluzianskya
    capensis, 41
    rubrostellata, 41
Zinnia
    angustifolia, 16, 90
    elegans, 6, 7
Zinnia, 94
    Creeping, 14–15
    Thread-Leaf, 16, 90

MICHAEL FUSCO

Brooklyn Botanic Garden

World renowned for pioneering gardening information, Brooklyn Botanic Garden's award-winning guides provide practical advice for gardeners in every region of North America.

Join Brooklyn Botanic Garden as an annual Subscriber Member and receive three gardening handbooks, delivered directly to you, each year. Other benefits include free admission to many public gardens across the country, plus four issues of *Plants & Gardens News, Members News,* and our guide to courses and public programs.

For additional information on Brooklyn Botanic Garden, including other membership packages, call 718-623-7210 or visit our web site at www.bbg.org. To order other fine titles published by BBG, call 718-623-7286 or shop in our online store at www.bbg.org/gardenemporium.

More Books on Fabulous Flowers